Reconciling Church Culture & Kingdom Culture

Reconciling Church Culture & Kingdom Culture

A Catalyst For Renaissance and Revival

CALVIN WILLIS

I.I.C. PUBLISHING
ATLANTA, GA.

Printed in the United States of America

Calvin Willis
"Reconciling Church Culture & Kingdom Culture: A Catalyst For Renaissance and Revival."

www.calvinwillis.com

ISBN: 978-0-578-60583-8 (print)

ISBN: 978-0-578-60584-5 (e-book)

Cover Design: Damascus Media

Editing: Daniel Johnson- Reedsy

Ordering Information:
Quantity sales. Special discounts are available on quantity purchases by corporations, associations, and others. For details, contact the publisher at the web address above.

Contents

Acknowledgements

First, I thank God for giving me endless love, grace and inspiration to accomplish anything in life.

With deepest appreciation:

- My wife Taniesha Willis for the sacrifice of love and helping edit some of the book. You are exceptional! Thank you for adding tremendous favor and blessings to my life. To our children Audia Willis and Calvin Willis, you bring me so much joy and are a blessing to this world!
- To my parents, Daphen Renee Willis and Calvin Willis. You are wonderful! Thanks for giving me the best of you and your constant support.
- To my siblings: Tabious Jackson, Tillie Mickens, Maurice Willis, April Willis, Isaac Mickens and Arin Willis, you are among the world's sharpest and brightest. Continue to let your light shine! To my nieces and nephews- I love you! Paris Jackson, Britain Levi Willis, Isaac Mickens & London Jackson. To my God sisters- Michan & Trisha, Lisa, much love!
- To my family: Willis, Sawyer, Rector, Eberhart, Howard, Collins, Snell, Miller, Roberson, Saxton, Gay, Jackson, David, Phillips, Shockley, Lockett, Wise and to all my cousins, aunts and uncles thank you for being strong, strong in love and support. Keep the faith!
- To my Grandparents: Samuel E. Sawyer a man of stature and favor, thank you! The late, Calvin and Sophia Willis and Tillie Rector all of your legacies live on!

- To my spiritual family: Embassy Church, Bryan and Patrice Meadows, Dominion World Outreach Center, Paul and Damita David & family, Fellowship Church of Praise, David and Vernette Rosier & family, Martin Street and every church that I have ever been a part of or served at, you are world changers set apart for times like these. TV & Eartha Drew & the Drew Family, New Life, Ekane Family and Foyere Family, may God continue to shine upon you!
- To Dr. William Ekane- thank you for writing the wonderful foreword for this book and providing marital counseling for my wife and me. You are a walking model of what God's love is.
- To my Friends and almamaters: Arkwright, Martin Street, Beecher Hills, Southwest, CCCS, Lindley, Pebblebrook, Fellowship Christian Academy, Florida A&M University- all my Famuly and Barney Fletcher, Keep Educating! To all the friends and teachers I met at these wonderful institutions and in life's journey, much love and keep being great!
- To all the churches and people of the earth who are spreading the good news of the Kingdom and helping people. Continue in God's strength!

- To my Work Family: SSA, GSA, Douglasville Conference Center, Jeff Justice & Co. Realtors, to all my real estate clients over the years and so many others, thank you for being a model of excellence and for your support!
- Thank you to Belinda Jackson & Picture it Possible for the "Harness the Wind" creative diagrams!
- Thank you Damascus Media for the awesome book cover design and marketing material!
- Thank you Jerrina Montgomery photography for the phenomenal branding images!
- Thank you Rod Brinson & Brinson Digital for the amazing web design!
- Thank you Daniel Johnson for the book editing!

Cali

IMAGINE. INSPIRE. CREATE.

Foreword

Foreword by Dr. William Ekane

I have read the manuscript of Pastor Calvin Willis' book "Reconciling Church Culture and Kingdom Culture – A Catalyst for Renaissance and Revival", and have been inspired and challenged by the depth, insights, and fresh approach to building a truly kingdom-minded church. Central to Calvin's core theological argument is that the extant church orthodoxy should be a reflection of the kingdom culture. In order, therefore, to reverse the status quo, the author provides persuasive answers to the following essential questions:

1. Where does kingdom culture begin?
2. Why do we need a renaissance and renewal in the body of Christ?
3. How do we encourage believers in Christ to worship Him in spirit and in truth without priming them?
4. What is the scriptural approach to reciprocal authority?
5. What are the specific mountains to be dismantled to bring about change in the body of Christ?
6. What approach must the church of Jesus Christ employ to revise, renovate, and rehabilitate the old system of doing church business?

It is my prayer that every Christian (especially our church leaders) study this book prayerfully and apply its principles in their lives and congregation.

Introduction

Since I was a young boy I have always loved the church. I can remember my mother taking me and my younger siblings to worship where I instantly fell in love with the music. I like to think of it as the first place to awaken the musical gifts deep inside my soul and spirit. I was drawn to the drums. I loved drums! Any chance I got after service or before I would go to the drum set and try to sit as close as I could to the musicians section. I watched the drummer meticulously every time. At home anything became my drum set: pots, pans, empty buckets, you name it. Most family functions you could find me playing basketball or playing drums. This "drumming on anything" habit was so pervasive that my Uncle Earl nicknamed me "Bambam" after the Flintstones cartoon character. They never let us young boys play the drums during the service, though I would always hope my time would come. Well, one day it almost did. It was a Wednesday night service at the Move of God Church in Atlanta; I was about 5 or 6 years old at the time. That night we were walking in and as soon as we made it in the front door, I darted full speed to the drum set. The praise team and the band were already in the middle of a song. When I reached the drummer, I attempted to take the sticks out of his hands so I could play. He laughed it off as my mother quickly came to his rescue and brought me to a seat. I was momentarily defeated, but my day did come later on, first with the youth choir and then eventually when I started to play regularly as a teenager and adult. It was through the church where I also developed a love for singing and writing music.

More importantly, it was there where I learned the discipline that comes with studying the Word of God. The seed of righteousness was planted in my heart because I heard the good news of the gospel preached and I repented of my sins and accepted Jesus Christ. In that moment I literally experienced the life of God transform me. I became a new person! Baptized in the name of the Father, Son & Holy Spirit! One of the greatest spiritual highs I've ever experienced was receiving the Holy Spirit with the evidence of speaking in tongues, and I have been using my prayer language, my heavenly language, till this day! From then on I have in turn preached to others, baptizing, discipling and teaching inside and outside of the church. I've seen miracles, signs and wonders. I have seen people's lives completely changed!!

In the midst of all this beauty and glory I've been a witness to over the years, in glaring juxtaposition are the things that I have experienced or observed that are detrimental and tend to stagnate our growth. In this book we will be discussing some of those things but not for the purpose of criticizing or "pointing the finger," but rather to teach, encourage and help the body of Christ to fully engage the message of the Kingdom. I struggled with many of the things I am going to write about and God has helped me to remove things that were in opposition to Kingdom culture being established in my life. God is still helping me with some of these things even today. These writings are in no way shape or form a negative criticism of any Pastor or church that I am or have been friends with. After my friend Dr. Ekane read the book, I asked him what he thought and did anything seem offensive? He said no, but that it challenged him. As a man who I highly respect as a Pastor, husband, father and author, this was very exciting to hear. It confirmed for me one of the primary reasons I wrote it had been accomplished. That's the way I want you to see this book, it is encouraging, empowering but also challenging.

The church is not adapting with the times at the pace it should or influencing what changes occur within the times. It is many of the rituals and traditions that remain the same for centuries that hinders our ability to change and make an impact. In this standoff of stagnation, we are forfeiting our power and influence. Why is this? Because by and large Church Culture is in opposition with

Kingdom Culture. Instead the church should be a reflection of the Kingdom of God. We are about to go on a journey of discovering how the Church and every other influencer of culture—Family, Business, Media, Arts & Entertainment, Government and Education—can go from being in opposition to being fully synchronized with Kingdom of God culture. As this happens, we will see Renaissance and Revival moving with an unbreakable anointing throughout the Nations. Every person, every family, every organization, every system and every nation is at its highest and best use when it has established a culture of the Kingdom. The purpose of this book is to help the body of Christ, the church and every other cultural influencer to establish a Kingdom mindset, thus producing a Kingdom of God culture. By doing this we bring God glory in the earth because this is His will for mankind. Thy Kingdom come, thy will be done on earth as it is in heaven.

Chapter 1: What is Kingdom Culture?

What is Kingdom?

In order to understand Kingdom culture we must first define the terms Kingdom and Culture. Kingdom is the word "basileia" and it means- royal power, kingship, dominion, and rule. The right or authority to rule over a territory. It is the royal power of Jesus as the triumphant Messiah. The royal power and dignity conferred on Christians in the Messiah's Kingdom. A territory subject to the rule of a King. I would like to briefly summarize the **Kingdom of God** as: **God's rule and reign**. It includes the **visible, invisible, tangible, intangible, heavens and the earth, every area of life and culture of society.** It is the reign of God over all things known, unknown, tangible, intangible, past, present and future. But the angel said to her, "do not be afraid, Mary; you have found favor with God. You will conceive and give birth to a son, and you are to call him Jesus. He will be great and will be called the Son of the Most High. The Lord God will give him the throne of his father David, and he will reign over Jacob's descendants forever; his Kingdom will never end" (Luke 1:30-33). Sending His son Jesus to earth is God's way of showing us what the Kingdom is and offering us an invitation into it. The highest honor in life is not to be an American citizen but a Kingdom citizen.

The scripture Colossians 1: 12-29 illuminates the crux of what the Kingdom is and what it means for us.

^{12} Giving thanks unto the Father, who has qualified you to share in the inheritance of his holy people in the kingdom of light.

¹³ Who hath **delivered us from the power of darkness, and hath translated us into the kingdom of his dear Son**:

¹⁴ In whom **we have redemption through his blood, even the forgiveness of sins:**

¹⁵ Who is the **image of the invisible God,** the firstborn of every creature:

¹⁶ For by him were all things created, that are **in heaven,** and that are **in earth, visible and invisible,** whether they be **thrones,** or **dominions,** or **principalities,** or **powers:** all things were created by him, and for him:

¹⁷ And he is before all things, and **by him all things consist.**

¹⁸ And **he is the head of the body, the church:** who is **the beginning,** the **firstborn** from the dead; that in **all things** he might have the **preeminence.**

¹⁹ For it pleased the Father that in him should all fulness dwell;

²⁰ And, having made **peace through the blood of his cross,** by him **to reconcile all things** unto himself; by him, I say, whether they be things **in earth,** or things **in heaven.**

²¹ And **you,** that **were sometime alienated** and **enemies** in your mind by wicked works, yet **now hath he reconciled**

²² In the **body of his flesh** through death, to present you **holy** and **unblameable** and **unreproveable in his sight:**

²³ If ye continue in the faith grounded and settled, and be not moved away from the hope of the gospel, which ye have heard, and which was **preached** to **every creature** which is under heaven; whereof I Paul am made a minister;

²⁴ Who now rejoice in my sufferings for you, and fill up that which is behind of the afflictions of Christ in my flesh for his body's sake, which is the church:

²⁵ Whereof I am made a minister, according to the dispensation of God which is given to me for you, to fulfil the word of God;

²⁶ **Even the mystery** which hath been **hid from ages and from generations,** but **now is made manifest** to his saints:

²⁷ To whom **God would make known** what is the **riches of the glory of this mystery** among the Gentiles; **which is Christ in you, the hope of glory:**

²⁸ Whom we **preach, warning** every man, and **teaching** every man in all **wisdom;** that we may present every man perfect in Christ Jesus:

²⁹ Whereunto I also labour, striving according to his working, which worketh in me mightily.

According to verse 13 were are translated from the power of darkness and "into the Kingdom." Later in verse 26 it talks about the mystery of the Kingdom that has now been revealed. The mystery revealed helps us define what being translated "into the Kingdom" means for us. Being in the Kingdom is when Christ the hope of glory is in you. The Pharisees asked Jesus when the Kingdom of God was coming? Jesus replied to them that it won't come with observation; people won't be able to say here it is or there it is, but the Kingdom of God is within you (Luke 17: 20-21). In other words, there won't be a physical takeover requiring tanks, missiles or military operations, but rather a New Birth whereby one is born again through repentance, the works of the Holy Spirit and believing in God through His Son Jesus Christ. If Christ the hope of glory is in me and I am a co-heir, a partaker in the Kingdom of God, where is the full manifestation of the Kingdom? You may be asking where is it in my life? Where is it within the church? There is one practical part of this that requires our cooperation in order for there to be manifestation of the Kingdom in us. It is found in verse 18 above: And he (Jesus) is the head of the body, the church, who is the beginning, the firstborn from the dead; that in all things he might have the **"preeminence."** Preeminence is from the word "proteuo" or "protos" and it means to be first, hold the first place, first in rank, influence and honor. As individuals do we acknowledge accept and embrace the preeminence of God through Jesus in every area of our lives? As the church do we acknowledge, accept and embrace the preeminence of God through Jesus in all that we do? Or have we settled for the label of "being saved" just to miss hell. I empathize because many of us were preached only a part of the gospel and came to Salvation just so we could not go to hell. But the vision of God for Salvation is so much more. Many have reduced Salvation to the confession with your mouth, but have not fully taught the believe with your heart portion. Belief and confession are coupled together for one to be saved. The process of Salvation in our minds seem to become two choices: confess with your mouth- Jesus is Lord i.e. sinner's prayer and then another choice to "make him Lord." However, it is only one choice "confess and believe." As we see in Colossians, Jesus is already Lord and has preeminence in all things. I understand it is a figure of speech but we can't "make Him Lord" He already is. Jesus has preeminence! We can choose to come into agreement and believe in his preeminence or not. It is the teaching of the belief in your heart that provides the template for us to manifest the Kingdom within. Romans 10: 9-10. If you declare with your mouth, "Jesus is Lord," and believe in your heart that God raised him from the dead, you will be saved. For it is with your heart that you believe and are justified, and it is with your mouth that you profess your faith and are saved. The disconnect is that many of us were not taught or choose not to believe that Jesus has preeminence or that He is Lord. Saying Jesus is Lord (has preeminence in every area of my life) and believing Jesus is Lord (has preeminence in every area of my life) are different things. Saying it without believing it does not activate the Kingdom within. Saying it is most effective when it comes as a result of first believing it. We have to believe it! Actions follow beliefs. Do we really believe it? How can you believe if you haven't heard it? How can you hear it without a preacher? Let us preach and teach the preeminence of God and the mystery that has now been made known, Christ in us, the hope of glory.

What is Culture?

Culture is the **customary beliefs**, social forms, and material traits of a racial, religious or social group. It is also the **shared attitudes**, **values**, **goals**, and **practices** that characterize an institution or organization. It is also enlightenment and excellence of taste acquired by intellectual and aesthetic training. Acquaintance with and taste in fine arts, humanities and broad aspects of science as distinguished from vocational and technical skills. I have also heard culture taught this way: thoughts create action, an action sustained creates an atmosphere, an atmosphere sustained creates climate and a climate sustained creates Culture. Therefore, culture is a sustained climate. What kind of culture do you want? Whether in business, in family or within church, the kind of climate that you not only initiate but sustain will determine your culture.

This word culture will help us to bridge the gap between two words in our subtitle, Renaissance and Revival. For example, you may hear a person say he or she is very cultured. In this sense of the definition, it is referring to the excellence of taste acquired by intellectual and aesthetic training. Aesthetic here means something pleasing in appearance; it's the beauty of a thing. For the most part in our experience, anyone proving cultured is labeled either "bad & bougie," or arrogant. In some cases they really could be arrogant and prideful, but not everyone who likes nice things, appreciates fine arts, cuisine and travel is bougie. We're supposed to want the best! Do you know that God created beautiful things that He placed in the earth just for our enjoyment? The perception that the church gives the world is that God is so serious, so in turn we become serious, and make our gatherings so serious. But God is a God of pleasure, laughter and enjoyment as well. This is why He gave us a need for it and we're made in His image. God gave us the desire and need to be cultured. The streets of heaven are paved with gold. If that isn't fine taste, I don't know what is. However, He wants us to have a proper perspective on this. We are not to accuse our brother or sister of being bougie just because they are cultured, and we should not become haughty or egotistical because God allowed us to increase our exposure. The Epicureans and Stoics Paul mentioned in the New Testament were a cultured people, very intellectual and lived in a time of great Renaissance. But God used Paul to preach the gospel of the Kingdom of God to them. Why? Because God loved them. He is a God of Revival and he is also a God of Renaissance. I will elaborate on this more as we go.

Kingdom Culture

Kingdom Culture is simply **God's way of doing things.** Kingdom of God Culture is also defined as God's rule and reign "established" in a person or organization. I use the term 'organization' very loosely as it derives from the root word 'organism', so in this way I am referring to everything living and breathing. On a macro level this could be the city/state you live in, the company you work for, the sorority or fraternity you're a part of, the school where your children attend, all the way down to the goldfish swimming in your 25 gallon aquarium. God cares about every part of your life, even the smallest things.

My family and I have a fish tank at home and a year ago we had goldfish. Well one of the goldfish died and like always it was a very sad occasion for the family. Shortly after, we decided to buy another goldfish to replace the one that died. We went into PetSmart and picked out a really cool looking goldfish with a white stripe on its body. We got home and put the goldfish in the tank, and at first it acted very erratically in the tank, which is normal for a new fish until it gets adjusted. When we noticed the fish was bullying and harassing the other two goldfish who were normally very peaceful and got along well, I still thought that maybe the fish just needed more time to adjust and then it would stop. I waited a few days to observe, but the new fish was still a bully. He would swim fast and ram into the two other fish, chase them around the tank and was just all around mean. Something had to be done about this to restore order. Then it hit me—I grabbed a tall empty flower vase from under the cabinet and filled it with water. Then I placed an oxygen line in the water, took the new fish and put it in the vase. It swam frantically after having been removed from the normal fish tank and placed in isolation. After a few hours it calmed down. I let the fish stay overnight in that makeshift tank. The next day I placed the fish back in the 25-gallon tank, and to my surprise he acted like a totally different fish. He was no longer aggressive or chasing and ramming the other fish. Instead, he peaceably swam and ate with them in our little family fish tank and the culture was restored. My wife and I observed in amazement at how that worked to restore the culture of our little family fish tank.

Everything in my house operates under Kingdom Culture, and that goes for the pets too. Kingdom Culture is established through discipleship. Matt 28:19 Go make disciples of all nations baptizing them in the name of the Father, Son and of the Holy Spirit, teaching them to obey everything I have commanded you. Our assignment is to preach and teach the Kingdom message to all the world. Why? In order to fulfill our purpose here on earth and because the Kingdom of God has a distinct message for every person, every culture, organization and system. When this is done according to God's will, Kingdom Culture will inevitably be established.

Jesus came to earth preaching and teaching the message of the Kingdom. One of the focuses of his ministry was reconciling every culture unto the Kingdom. I'd like to explore a few places in scripture that further explain this.

Power, Authority & Healing

Luke 9: 1-6: Summoning the Twelve, He gave them power and authority over all demons, and the power to heal diseases. Then He sent them to proclaim the Kingdom of God and to heal the sick. "Take nothing for the road," He told them, "no walking stick, no traveling bag, no bread, no money; and don't take an extra shirt. Whatever house you enter, stay there and leave from there. If they do not welcome you, when you leave that town, shake off the dust from your feet as a testimony against them." So they went out and traveled from village to village, proclaiming the good news and healing everywhere.

First we have to note that the disciples were being sent out to establish Kingdom Culture. They were given power and authority. Whose power and authority were they given? Because they certainly were not operating out of their own. They were given authority from God through Jesus Christ. This gives them the ability to act on His behalf. Just like God shows up through Jesus in the earth, Jesus shows up through us in the earth. He is present through you. What were the two primary assignments of their call and commission? It was to exert power and authority over demons, also known as strongholds. A demon or stronghold is an evil spirit in or around a person that influences their thoughts, actions or behavior.

Have you ever heard stories of people who hear voices telling them that they're a failure or that they should kill themselves or kill someone else? In many cases this is an indication of an evil spirit at work. However, this is not true in all cases. Not every thought of this nature is the result of a demon. For example, someone who may get angry or exhibit signs of depression. Sometimes we are just thinking the wrong thoughts. Depression is thinking about the wrong thing too long and the problem is that when you think about the wrong thing for too long, it's like sending out an invitation for a demon to join you. The good news is that God knows when you're vulnerable, and He says that He is close to the brokenhearted. He also gives us guidance on how we should think. Whatsoever things are noble, admirable, noteworthy, think on these things.

The mind is the biggest battlefield, but you have victory there! We know of 14 strongholds mentioned in scripture, and Jesus had authority over each one of them. The second assignment was to heal diseases. Jesus said deliverance is the children's bread. Many of us have thought deliverance is complete once the demon is cast out, but that is only one part. You are delivered out and delivered to, just like when the mailman delivers a piece of mail to your home—out from the post office where it had to be processed and into your home where you are the recipient. Hallelujah! He is delivering you out of captivity and into destiny. Healing completes the deliverance process because once you are set free, you still have a destiny to reach. You still have a world to set ablaze for the Kingdom of God. Your healing makes you a blessing to those who will be a recipient of the grace that's in your life. Oh beloved, that you may prosper and be in good health even as your soul prospers.

The "Do Not Pack" List.

And so, the disciples went village to village full of healing power! This is where it gets a little perplexing. They're about to go on a journey for miles, days, even months and Jesus tells them what not to pack. Most times when we go on just a short weekend trip, we make a pack list or at least a mental one. Jesus has a do not pack list. On the "do not pack list" are the following (I can imagine Jesus clearing His throat here):

No walking stick

No traveling bag (we call that a suitcase or toiletry bag)

No bread

No money

No extra shirt

A "Go Belt" (@itsgobelt) would have been great for them since Jesus wanted them to be hands free with no distractions. But His do not pack list included pretty much everything we would think we'd need for the journey. When I looked at it, I had to ask, "Why didn't He want them to take those items?" I think this shows that God wanted them to understand He Is all of these things for them. His name is **JEHOVAH JIREH – "The Lord Will Provide"** and if they are going to know Him as The Provider, The Provision, they have to have firsthand experience.

There are many things in our lives that are discovered through faith-filled movement and not just being told step by step what to do. I am in a season of experiencing that right now in my own life. What I have found is that it feels like indecisiveness, and I have never been an indecisive person. What's really happening is that God has given me a "do not pack" list, and the only things on this list are the things I'm most familiar and comfortable with. God has also given the church a do not pack list and it too is full of the things we're most comfortable and familiar with. Much like the disciples, He is re-calibrating our soul and spirit to rely on Him for everything completely.

A walking stick is used for protection to fight off stray animals and wild dogs, climb hills and mountains and cross a body of water. But they didn't need a walking stick, because He Is **YAHWEH ROHI- "The Lord Our Shepherd."** A shepherd is one who guides, who protects and takes great care of his sheep. Just as a shepherd cares for his sheep, the Lord takes extreme care of us as his people. This next scripture depicts how God the good shepherd takes care of us. These are the words from someone who came to intimately know Him as YAHWEH ROHI. The Lord is my shepherd; I shall not want. He makes me to lie down in green pastures; He leads me beside the still waters. He restores my soul, He leads me in the paths of righteousness for His name's sake. Yea though I walk through the valley of the shadow of death, I will fear no evil; for You are with me; Your rod and Your staff, they comfort me. You prepare a table before me in the presence of mine enemies; You anoint my head with oil; my cup runs over. Surely goodness and mercy shall follow me all the days of my life and I will dwell in the house of the Lord forever. I believe the reason for no walking stick is because If God is our shepherd, he leads, guides and protects alleviating the need for us to do it on our own. Say this prayer with me, Lord I want to know you as YAHWEH ROHI. I give myself permission to be helped, guided and protected.

A traveling bag, money, bread and an extra shirt are all the things you need to stay refreshed on a journey. Here they will understand him to be **YAHWEH-SHAMMAH – "The Lord Is There."** Your past, He is there! Your present, He is there! Your future, He is there! The reason Jesus can so confidently call out the do not pack list is because He is already in the place they're going. God is omnipresent and is already in their future and worked out those minor details. I want to announce to you that God has gone into your future and worked out all the details! On top of that, He owns it all—houses, cars, land; all of these are things we are given the privilege to manage on His behalf. He already had houses, clothes, money, and an extra shirt stored up for them in the place of their assignment. All they had to do was show up! Since they're not worrying about those things, their minds are free of all those encumbrances and available to commune with God. Jesus directly tells us, do not worry about what to wear, eat or drink. Just like He takes care of the birds of the air, how much more will He take care of me.

Lastly, Matthew 6:33 says to seek ye first the Kingdom and his righteousness and all these things will be added unto you. Did it say seek ye first your marriage? No, the Kingdom. Seek ye first your church? The Kingdom!!! Seek ye first your business? The Kingdom!!! Seek ye first politics? Seek ye first monetary gain? Nope. The Kingdom!!!

Leave The 99

It is the glory of God to conceal a matter and the glory of Kings to search it out. Luke 15 is one of my favorite chapters which illustrates the diligence and value of seeking and joy of recovering what was lost. It depicts how three different things that were lost, but found.

The first story is where the shepherd leaves his 99 sheep in an open field to go after one lost sheep. When he finds it, he joyfully puts the sheep on his shoulder and calls his friends and neighbors to celebrate. This act of putting the sheep on the shoulder is symbolic of order being restored. This is a principle that I have lost sight of at times, just as the church as a whole has. How many times have we watched people wander off and never even stopped to ask what happened & why they left? In many cases, there isn't a sense of urgency about a lost or wandering soul, but more of an interest in continuing with "business as usual." We have a "nothing can disrupt the flow of the service" mentality because we don't want to ever appear as though we don't have it all together. Dear friends, this mentality is on the do not pack list. Kingdom Culture says there are built-in times where you are going to look like you don't have it together. In the story of the one lost sheep, the shepherd, who is symbolic of the senior Pastor, the Senior Leader went looking for someone who had gone back into sin and left those who were saved for a while. This may appear to men that you don't have it all together. But are you more concerned about man's perception of you or God's?

Even when you don't understand what's happening, you do have it together because you're in God and He has it together. We've got to start going after people. Make the call, go ride to where they live or where you know they will be. Sometimes I will just ride down the streets where I know one of my loved ones is known for hanging out in hopes that I can find them and minister the love of the Father to them. Go after your loved ones. Do what it takes, make the sacrifice. Pastors, go after those who have left and are lost. Do not just wait on them to return to you. There is more joy in heaven over one sinner who repents than over 99 who don't need repentance. Celebrate Big when they come home!

The second parable says, The Kingdom of Heaven is like a treasure that a man discovered hidden in a field. In his excitement, he hid it again and sold everything he owned to get enough money and bought that field. In the third parable, one woman had 10 silver coins; she lost one. Then she lit a lamp, swept the house and when she found it, she called up her girls and neighbors saying "Come rejoice with me, I have found the silver coin I lost." In the same way there is joy in the presence of God's angels over one sinner who repents.

Are you starting to see the pattern here? Not over the lost and found, but over the celebration that happens when a person who was in sin is found by grace. Do you see how much heaven is keeping track of what is happening here? To rejoice and celebrate every time one sinner repents! I know it's hard to fathom, but it is true. I know that praise and worship is going on perpetually in heaven because of the absolute Holiness of God. Just because of the overwhelming glory, awe and majesty of **EL SHADDAI – God Almighty.** We know this. However, this is a place where I see it repeatedly, explicitly mentioned in scripture that heaven celebrates as a result of something that happens here in the earth. They are celebrating because Isaiah 6:3 says and they were calling to one another: Holy, Holy, Holy is the Lord Almighty; the whole earth is full of His glory. God so loved us that He sent His son Jesus to die on the cross and resurrect on the third day to redeem us from sin. Every time a sinner repents, His glory fills the earth. Heaven and earth has no choice but to respond to His glory. Let's be conduits for that glory and rejoice with Heaven. Being a conduit will require the undivided seeker in you. What is that part of you that seeks and, like the man in the parable, will gladly sell everything you have and invest yourself fully because you have found the Greater One? As you seek and find, the glory of the Lord fills your life as it fills the earth!

Chapter 2: What is Church Culture?

What is Church?

Church comes from the word **Ekklesia**– an assembly of Christians gathered for worship; a **called out assembly united as one body.** The church is a spiritual family known as the people of God and the bride of Christ. The church is made up of many denominations, races and socioeconomic groups from all over the world. Since we are one body, when I speak of the Church, I am referring to the church at large.

For a long time we have thought of and acted as though the Church and the Kingdom are the same. On the contrary, the church is in the Kingdom and the Kingdom is in the Church. The church is to be an expression of and representative of the Kingdom of God, but it is not the only expression. The Kingdom is vast, limitless and without end. (Luke 1:33). It stretches far beyond what is visible or tangible to you and I here on earth.

Church Culture

Church Culture then is the way things are done within the church. From customary beliefs, to shared attitudes, values, rituals and traditions, all of these create the culture of the church and its way of doing things. It is a **climate of sustained rituals and traditions.** What I will be addressing in particular throughout this book are the "empty religious practices" that for centuries have become a driving force in Church Culture. The problem is that many of these rituals and traditions are void of the Holy Spirit's direction but instead operate on man's autopilot setting. "We did it this way last year, so we're doing it this way again." "God met us when we did it like this last Sunday, so we're doing it this Sunday."

Church culture should be a reflection of Kingdom culture. They should be interwoven like a beautiful tapestry or a quilt that covers you in the coldest winter, embroidered with words that warm your spirit and give life. For this to happen, the two must be reconciled into one. If an accountant is putting together a financial statement and finds themselves off by one dollar, the process of finding that missing dollar is what they call "reconciling the account." Once they find the missing dollar, they can give an accurate statement and the account is reconciled. Think of reconciling Church Culture and Kingdom culture this same way. We're off by a certain amount, except in this case our amount is not in dollars but the number of people we don't see, unity we don't have, miracles we haven't witnessed, disciples we haven't made or communities that have seen no transformation. The word 'reconcile' here means to restore friendly relations between, to cause to coexist in harmony, to be compatible, to make congruent, to be in agreement and to make one account. Once Church Culture (the way we've known it) and Kingdom Culture (the way God envisioned it to be) are reconciled, we will experience Renaissance and Revival. Now, let's define these two terms.

Renaissance is a **cultural re-birthing**. Imagine the new birth experience happening to an entire culture of influence. Imagine the culture of Arts and Entertainment baptized into Kingdom of God creativity. What better creative to draw inspiration from than the Creator Elohim? Renaissance can also be defined as a revival of renewed interest in something. Interest is the state of wanting to know or learn about something or someone. All of creation, whether they recognize it or not have a growing interest in the creator Elohim and His people. The whole earth is groaning in anticipation for the true sons and daughters to arise. As much as it seems like the world is falling away from God, there is a growing interest and need for the Kingdom of God to come. As a business term, interest also means "stake." To have a stake in something means you have a vested interest in something or someone. God has a stake, an interest in everything in heaven and on earth, but more specifically, in you and I and every culture of influence. He has a stake because He created us and sent His Son Jesus Christ to give His very life for us. God has an interest in every culture and certainly there is a message that speaks to each one specifically that we are going to journey through. Though Renaissance is also defined as the revival of art and literature under the influence of classical models in the 14th-16th centuries, I don't believe it stopped there. It's happening right now in hip-hop culture, pop culture, music, dance, art, film, education, policy making and many more.

Now let's define revival. **Revival** comes from the root word **'revive'** which means to **restore to life or consciousness.** The word revive is mentioned in scripture seven times. Seven is the number of completion and rest. God wants us to have a holistic approach when it comes to revival. Revival is an improvement in the condition or strength of something, an instance of something becoming popular, active or important again. I like to further define it as revitalized influence and power. In "School of Revival," Bryan Meadows defines Revival as the normalization of Kingdom Culture. There is no revival apart from the One who gives life.

Church culture as we know it today looks almost nothing like what we read about in the New Testament. In that day people went house to house, breaking bread and building each other up in the faith. Everyone had a praise, psalm, hymn or something to edify the group. Then we had the dinner table, communion and discipleship through active participation. Today we have traded that for the praise team, one Pastor and a stage. What we call discipleship has been reduced to a myriad of classes where, for the most part, one person speaks and participants take notes. It mirrors nothing of the three year experience the disciples had up close and personal with Jesus where they learned through various ways, like traveling from place to place with ministry, teaching, observing it being done, trial & error, doing it themselves and success.

I am not saying discipleship classes are ineffective. In fact, they are a great tool for training and teaching. I have attended many great classes over the years, growing spiritually and personally, and I was thoroughly trained and developed. However, classes alone are just one style of teaching when there are many more that Jesus shows us that are at our disposal. My purpose is to challenge us to rethink why we're doing it the way we are and how we're doing it. I am encouraging everyone to ask the Lord: What is the best way for us to be disciples? Are you doing it the way you're doing it because that's the way you've always known it to be? Was it handed down to you and you just figured it works because other people did it this way? Or have you inquired of the Lord on new and innovative ways that are unique to your gifts and personality? We need to challenge old patterns that have been handed down for decades. Just because it was done then doesn't mean it should be done the same now. It's time to rethink why we do what we do and how we do what we do.

The Praise Team, The Pastor And The Stage

Of course, there is nothing wrong with having a praise team, Pastor or stage. It is the method of how we use it that contributes to a predictability that blunts the sharpness of our relevance and influence. People know what's going to happen before it happens. We know the praise team will do two fast songs, one slow, preach, take up an offering and go home—week after week after week. This is one reason why people are not coming to our gatherings anymore. (Notice I didn't say coming to church anymore, but we'll talk more about that later.) This cycle of predictability and non-engagement creates a culture of spectators. Instead of engaging, sharpening their character and gift, congregations are sitting, watching the people on stage sharpen their gift while they drift into spectating. A culture of spectators does not create disciples. If disciples are not being created, people are stuck on the first level of Salvation where they have only begun a relationship with God but are not operating in the full authority and power made available to them by the finished works of Jesus and being a citizen of the Kingdom. This is the danger of moving away from Kingdom Culture. I Corinthians 14:6 says when you come together each one of you has a hymn, or a word of instruction, a revelation, a tongue of interpretation. Everything must be done so that the church may be built up. The principle found in this scripture alleviates the spectating culture, allows everyone to be discipled and utilize their faith and gift. The most common rebuttal I hear to implementing this scripture is: it would take forever to do that. We dismiss this before giving it the thought and proactiveness it needs in order to implement it. Spectating and "having good church" is what we have become comfortable with but how is that changing my life or the lives of the people God has called me to?

Why do Pastors and Leaders create cultures of spectatorship then get mad at the people for being this way? We then think the barometer for people really being engaged is how loud they yell Amen and how much they obey the Worship Leader who barks praise commands. A person could yell Amen at the top of their lungs, obey every praise leader command and still be unengaged. Why? Because that's Church Culture, it has nothing to do with the Kingdom. Scripture says man looks on the outward appearance, but God looks on the heart. You're watching for a person's outward response and the whole time it's about what's happening in the parts you can't see: the heart, soul and spirit. As Pastors, we must take responsibility for what we know, didn't know and some of the places we have led the people. God is not condemning us but giving us an opportunity to transition into something greater! It is time to delegate leadership and authority and get back to a discipleship experience founded in true relationship, not confined by buildings but moving, active, going place to place.

See One, Do One, Teach One

See One, Do One, Teach One is a principle for surgical training in the medical field. I'm fascinated at how different cultures of influence give us examples of ways their culture can be reconciled with Kingdom Culture. See One, Do One, Teach One is certainly a Kingdom culture mentality. The thought is if you see a surgery, you do one and then teach one. This strategy dismantles a culture of the non-discipleship which creates spectators and is one of the most effective ways of teaching for the mentor and learning for the mentee. What if a surgeon only chose to observe his or her mentor doing surgeries but never did one themselves? Would that doctor be considered a surgeon? They implemented this principle because as a resident they would follow their mentor and watch the surgeries, if they watched the mentor perform more than one surgery, the intern would become intimidated by the complexity of the work. But if you see one, do one and then teach one, it boosted the young doctor's confidence.

We know this is a Kingdom principle because when Jesus showed His disciples how to preach, teach, heal, and do miracles, he gave them the opportunity to do the same. They even had a chance to ask why their method didn't work. They wanted to know why when they prayed for a demon to be cast out, it didn't leave? Jesus told them because this kind only comes out through prayer and fasting. But let's focus on the disciples asking Jesus why they're method wasn't working because this is where the church is. Some of our methods are not working and we need to ask the Lord why. It is not a time to be in denial that our methods aren't working or a time to become prideful. Are we humble enough to ask God why our methods are not working or how they could work better? If the answer is yes, then read on—you are ready for Renaissance and Revival!

Rituals and Traditions of Men

Church culture now rarely reflects what Jesus said we could have and who we could be. Jesus said that greater signs shall follow them that believe. In my opinion, our full potential is not being realized because church culture is operating more on the rituals and traditions of men than on the gospel of the Kingdom. Mark 7: 6-9 and 13 says, these people honor me with their lips, but their hearts are far from me. They worship me in vain; their teachings are merely human rules. You have let go of the commands of God, for you are holding on to human traditions. And he continued, you have a fine way of setting aside the commands of God in order to observe your own traditions. 13- thus you nullify the word of God (making it to no effect) by your own tradition that you have handed down. And you do many things like that. Many people have made an idol out of church, church traditions and even their Pastor. An idol is anything you put before God. You give it first place instead of God.

Here is another reference in Matthew 15:9 of when good man made ideas become commands- And in vain they worship me, teaching as doctrines the commandments of men. Let's talk about the word vain. It means unsuccessful, fruitless and manipulation. When we become a culture of man-made traditions, God says our worship is unsuccessful and fruitless. Worship is supposed to produce fruit. How? When it is done in spirit and in truth- not when it's done because this is the way it's always been. When I say worship I am not just referring to a song you sing with the church on Sunday. I'm talking about the posture of your heart toward God every day in every situation. God said in Mark 7, the scripture above, they honor me with their lips but their hearts are far from me. Everything in life, especially worshiping and pleasing God, is always a matter of the heart. Relying on our man made culture and tradition is also a matter of the heart. Do we do it because we are fearful of change? Or is it because our hearts are not fully postured toward God so we can hear and see what is next? Is it because this way of doing it provides the most comfort, money or notoriety? Whatever the reason is, it all stems from the heart. Before we can reconcile every culture to the Kingdom, we have to first allow God to reconcile each and every heart.

If you have ever said or thought to yourself this is the way it will always be. Or if you operate out of a place where even when you find something good that God supplied as a provision and say this is what I'll always have or how I'll always operate chances are, you have slipped into man made traditions. The bible says we are to be led by the spirit. The spirit moves like the wind—you can't tell where it came from or where it's going next. We must have this same mindset as God leads us day by day on where and how to lead His church. God shows what we should do in this season and when He shows you follow. The children of Israel needed the cloud by day and the fire by night when they were wandering in the desert. Those two natural elements had a significant purpose for the season they were in. The cloud moved, providing shade which gave them a direction to go in and respite from the sweltering heat so they wouldn't pass out on the way there. The fire was to keep them warm at night because the desert is a place of extremes. It gets really hot during the day and really cold at night. They didn't need the cloud and the fire once they entered the Promised Land. But what if they tried to manipulate and hold on to what God had used in a previous season? God needed them to adjust to the next provision and set of instructions, but if they were stuck on how he moved in the desert, they would have missed it. It is tragic to be in a mode of continuously bringing God something He no longer needs and expecting Him to continuously give you something you no longer need.

I'm here to encourage you that God wants the shift to start with you. As the spirit moves, I see you beginning to move. There is a specific blueprint for what God wants you to build. I pray that He speaks to you and you hear very clearly as God gives you a vision of your blueprint. Years of your life will be recovered if you have been building in vain and did not know it. There is a Kingdom Cycle of acceleration that God is instituting on your behalf. It is unique to your personality and you will no longer experience the dichotomy of changing your personality to fit into ministry or the church. The anointing God gave you works when you talk like you, walk like you and act like yourself. A renaissance of authenticity is hitting every culture where we are no longer ashamed of where we've been, but are bold and confident in who we are. Your worship will be fruitful and successful because you are moving into doing it God's way.

Chapter 3: Church Culture -vs- Kingdom Culture

Methods

In the Kingdom of God, the method is as important as the objectives. God has a message for both issues. He so desperately wants to influence what we do and how we do it. Why? Because how we do it has a direct impact on our results and effectiveness. If you had a road trip planned from Atlanta to California and had the option to drive a Model T- Ford (one of the first cars ever made) or a Tesla, which one would you choose? Of course! The Tesla! You could choose the Model T, but it wouldn't be fast enough, able to keep up or outpace today's method of travel. Why then do we hold on to outdated methods of ministry, preaching, reaching the lost or discipleship? Just because that method was used then doesn't mean He's using it now. However, the principle remains, you have a destiny to reach and a Heavenly Father to make proud by using the objectives and methods He has given you. Adam and Eve eating the fruit. Moses striking the rock. In Ai, God said leave everything but Achan still took some of the spoils with him. Jesus had disciples to make the people sit down in groups before they were fed. The Ten Virgins and the lamp. All of these events are important to understanding that God is interested in both the method and the objective.

I was recently on the bus and there was a little girl happily singing a song on her way to school as she sat next to her Mom. After a few minutes the mom grew weary of the little girl's singing and abruptly told her, "The song is over!" In other words, stop singing and be quiet. Why did she tell her to stop? The little girl was just showing her happiness and wasn't bothering anybody. She then gave the little girl her cellphone to quiet her down. The little girl seemed to aggravate the mom more at this point because she couldn't find anything on the phone to keep her entertained. The mom then yelled at her and the little girl became sad and sat there with the hood of her coat halfway over her face. At this point I heard, the mom say "Don't hit me," right before aggressively smacking the little girl across the face with almost the same force you would expect someone to hit another adult. This little girl was about three years old. I was furious! After contemplating for a few minutes how I would confront the lady, I went for it. "Excuse me Ma'am what is your name? She replied. "Well I noticed first that you told her "the song is over" while she was singing and being happy. I was enjoying her song by the way. Now look at her countenance, she is sad. Then you smack her in the face. How did it make you feel when your mother smacked you in the face in public?!" She gave me a look as if to say "how did you know that?" At this point the lady was upset me and became very combative. She then said, "I tell you what, do you want her?" "Because you can have her." Speaking of her own daughter. That's why kids are beating up parents now, because the parents put up with that kind of stuff. I replied to her "Ma'am, there are other ways to discipline. You could have communicated that to her."

After our heated discussion, she asked the bus driver to get off. It did not end with any conspicuous compromise, but I pray a seed was planted. I mention that story because it is a prime example of simply doing what was done to you. The woman didn't have to tell me her mother smacked her in the face in public when she was growing up. I knew it because most of us only do what was done to us, and she had to learn this behavior somewhere. She thought that just because she survived it that it was worth implementing in her parenting method. Just because you survived it doesn't mean it should be implemented as your methodology. This is not just true when it comes to the church but other areas. Parenting is one of them. How many times do you see the parents who only seem to use the method of yelling and spanking when it comes to disciplining children? By default, this way of parenting gets handed down and re-implemented because we figure, "Well, I turned out okay, I survived it, so it must have worked." We seldom take the time to analyze how those experiences of what happened to us or didn't happen to us had an effect on how we think or behave as an adult.

What many of us survive is dysfunction, abuse and neglect, and as long as we don't confront it, the cycle will continue. Confrontation is not a bad word. If we are going to implement Kingdom Culture, we must be willing to engage the culture through confrontation. If you are reading this, you are about to disrupt cycles of dysfunction through confrontation. It's time to become disruptive! Disruptive Intercession! Disruptive Preaching & Teaching! Disruptive Praise & Worship! Disruptive conversations!

Church Culture -vs- Kingdom Culture

Church Culture is in opposition with Kingdom Culture. The problem with this statement is that it's only supposed to be one culture. Kingdom Culture. In a marriage is there one head of household or two? Jesus is the groom, the church is the bride. Who is the head? Jesus! Isn't it interesting that this is the same struggle that exists in a marriage? The wife wants her way of doing things—she wants her culture and the husband has his way of doing things and wants to establish his culture. It was the same struggle when Jesus was handed over to Pontius Pilate before He was crucified and Pilate asked the people who should he let go free Jesus or Barabbas? The people replied, "Give us Barabbas!" Yeah they knew he was a thief and a murderer, but they also knew what to expect and felt more comfortable sticking with an old system of corruption rather than choosing this Jesus who says He is the Son of God and talking about a Kingdom not of this world. Barabbas represented an old system, while Jesus represented the new system. Barabbas represents an empty church culture while Jesus represents Kingdom Culture.

Can't we have both cultures working together at the same time? Any culture not aligned with Kingdom culture will breed corruption and miss the mark. It will be hard for the body of Christ to progress until we reconcile the two, because this reconciliation was an important part of Jesus' ministry.

Let's take a look at some specific things that I believe are "empty" church culture practices. Empty means lacking guidance by the Holy Spirit, something done out of error or man-made tradition. I'm not saying if your church practices any of these that your entire church culture is unhealthy. I'm just saying if you don't stop practicing these unhealthy habits, your church culture will likely become unhealthy.

On the next few pages you will see the Church Culture -vs- Kingdom Culture chart. Empty Church Culture practices are on the left and the opposite attributes of Kingdom Culture are on the right.

Church Culture -vs- Kingdom Culture

Empty Church Culture	Kingdom Culture
Classism- If you don't have much money, power or respect, people ignore or place less value on you.	Do not be proud, but be willing to associate with people of low position. Do not be conceited. Be devoted to one another in love. Honor one another above yourselves. Share with the Lord's people who are in need. Practice Hospitality. (Romans 12:9-16).
Racism- the culture, form of worship, preaching, singing from my ethnic group is better than all others.	God so loved the "world' that He gave His only begotten Son (John 3:16). Do not call anything impure that God has made clean (Acts 10:1-48). People are saved by faith (Galatians 2:11-21). You are no more strangers and foreigners, but fellow citizens with the saints and the household of God (Ephesians 2:19-22). In Christ we who are many are one body, and each member belongs to one another (Romans 12:5).

Exclusivity- if you don't do it like we do it you are not accepted, included, placed in high esteem or honored.	To the praise of the glory of His grace, we are accepted in the beloved. (Ephesians 1:1-14). Knowledge puffs up but love builds up. (I Corinthians 8:1-3)
Dancing with no joy or revelation but rather because it's a religious ritual.	Let them praise his name with dancing and make music to him (Psalms 149:3). Not to see who can do it the best or because a certain chord is played. After we have reaped the rewards as a result of doing the type of fasting described here in Isaiah, then we will delight in the Lord and He will cause us to ride upon the high places of the earth (Isaiah 58:1-14).
Many rituals but no power, results or transformation.	Leave your gift at the altar, first go and be reconciled to your brother, then come and offer your gift (Matthew 5:24).
Worships out of a programmatic system, i.e. Simon says worship but lacks true intimacy.	I don't want your sacrifices, I want your love; I don't want your offerings, I want you to know me (Hosea 6:6). They honor me with their lips but their hearts are far from me. They worship me in vain, their teachings are mere human rules. You have let go of the commands of God and are holding on to human traditions (Mark 7: 5-13)

Upset when people leave the church, speak negative words or curses, never ask why they left, do not celebrate them or maintain fellowship. Also rarely goes after the one who left.	Wherever you go and whatever you do, you will be blessed. Blessed coming in, blessed going out (Deuteronomy 28:6). God builds His church- (Matthew 16:18), these are God's people not your people. You are entrusted to manage what is God's & love them as He would. Stop being offended when they leave. The belief that a person has to belong to one local church their entire lives is a man-made rule and expectation. Change your definition and expectations of "church membership". We should possibly even get rid of our current "church membership" category because of the possessive connotation that comes along with it. As believers, we are members of the household of faith, the family of God, citizens of the Kingdom and God's church. Go will be bringing people in and deploying them as He chooses. Corporate America has enough honor intelligence to celebrate employees when they leave and even do surveys or exit interviews to see why they left and get feedback, yet the church can't find it within themselves to celebrate, honor or get insight from believers who carry the spirit of the living God.
Equip and train the church but never deploy.	Jesus sent them "out" 2×2 to do the works of ministry. (Luke 10: 1-12), (Mark 6: 6-8). Go make disciples of all nations. (Matt 28: 18-20)
Creates spectators & reinforces spectating culture. (Dependency on Pastor & Praise Team).	When you come together each of you has a hymn, or word of instruction, a revelation, a tongue or an interpretation (I Corinthians 14:26).

We have songwriters, singers & creatives but seldom embrace originality through new songs & creativity.	God created man in his own image (Genesis 1:27). We have this treasure in earthen vessels (2 Corinthians 4:7).
Youth and Young Adults are activated or acknowledged only on "Youth Sunday," easter speech or the Christmas play.	From the mouths of children and infants you have ordained praise on account of your adversaries to silence the enemy and avenger (Psalm 8:2). Let the little children come unto me, and do not hinder them. For the Kingdom of heaven belongs to such as these. (Matthew 19:14) Why did Jesus say "such as these?" Because (Matthew 18:2) tells us unless you change and become like little children, you will never enter the Kingdom of heaven. We have a lot to learn from the youth.
Control and manipulation through the offering or withdrawal of acceptance. Acceptance is only offered if you give, submit, stay loyal & sacrifice. If not, acceptance is withdrawn and rejection is given.	Accept one another, then, just as Christ accepted you, in order to bring glory to God (Romans 15:17). Christ offered us acceptance and love while we were still sinners.
Unrealistic expectation of "church attendance."	What sorrow awaits you experts in religious law! For you crush people with unbearable religious demands, and you will never lift a finger to ease the burden (Luke 11:46).
Church attendance most closely equals Kingdom Business.	For I have come down from heaven to do the will of the one who sent me. (John 6:38). This is the same reason we are sent here. Doing the will of the one who sent us does include ministry within the church but it is not the totality of His will. We are called to do ministry in nations, families, systems & organizations as God leads.

Church Hopping & the gossip culture.	Those that be planted in the house of the Lord, they will flourish in the courts of our God (Psalm 92:13). A perverse person stirs up conflict, and a gossip separates close friends (Proverbs 16:28).
More focused on financing physical buildings than the actual temples which are God's people.	Do you not know that you yourselves are God's temple, and that God's spirit dwells in you (I Corinthians 3:16). The God who made the world and everything in it is the Lord of heaven and earth and does not live in temples built by human hands (Acts 17:24).
Enjoys titles and feels potential for disrespect by those "under" them if not called by that title.	They love to be greeted with respect in the marketplaces and to be called 'Rabbi' by others. But you are not to be called 'Rabbi,' for you have one Teacher, and you are "all" brothers. And do not call anyone on earth Father, for you have one Father, and He is in heaven. (Matthew 23: 5-12). In other words, your Pastor, Apostle, Bishop, spiritual father or mother is still your brother or sister in Christ. Church leaders should not be so enamored with titles and making other people call you by that title. Stop treating people like they are subservient to you. You are brothers, sisters, co-laborers and friends; there is no hierarchy.

Church Attendance ≠ Kingdom Culture

Church attendance does not equal adherence to Kingdom Culture. Many churches often make people feel like if they aren't willing to attend 5 days a week, every event or stay for long hours, they are not serious about GOD. This ends up forming cliques among those who stay committed to the long hours and 5 days a week. When this culture begins to form, we appear to be cultish. If we don't want to be perceived as a cult, we have to stop acting like them as it relates to this type of behavior.

If you have events which you expect people to attend 5 to 6 nights a week, when do people have time to:

1.) Cultivate their personal relationship with God

2.) Cultivate relationships with family and friends

3.) Make new friends

4.) Make disciples- build relationships, mentor

5.) Evangelize- do works of ministry or do the work of an Evangelist.

What I just described to you is lifestyle evangelism, which I will talk about in more detail in a later chapter. This method of 'doing church' directly impedes our ability to do lifestyle evangelism and just enjoy life! Church Leadership will say we understand if you can't make it to everything. But the minute you enforce your boundary of not attending everything to live a balanced life, many begin treating you different by showing less respect, less honor and an attitude of indifference.

Jesus Has Left the Building

Jesus Has Left the Building, *by Paul Vieira* is a book that totally challenged and reaffirmed my way of thinking on our connection to the church. For centuries we have thought of the building as the place where God dwelled. Now, this used to be true, but God changed His method just as He predestined. Jesus, the living word came down, was crucified, died and rose on the third day. Once Jesus ascended and went back to the Father, God sent us His spirit on the day of Pentecost in Acts 2. This forever changed our relationship to a physical building. After this point, buildings and temples were not the carriers of His presence and glory. Our spirits are the place where the spirit of God now dwells. We are his temple. Therefore, our relationship and perception of buildings must change. Our connection to the church is not because we go to a church building, but because we are the church.

Buildings are simply a tool and technology God gives us to carry out our mission. However, it seems as though we are so dependent on them that nothing can happen outside of them. The method of most church plants is centered around finding a building. The goal of established churches is to find a bigger and better building. Our current church culture is trying to get into buildings, while Jesus is trying to get out of the building. He's trying to get you out of the building. The financial obligation of a building affects what we do and how we do it as a church. For example, if we have a big financial burden as a result of acquiring a building, we will likely host more events at the building to pay for the building. There will be more money allocated to fund facility operations & maintenance than the ministry assignments God told us to fund: helping the poor, orphans and widows, homeless, believers who have a need. We must reconcile this into a Kingdom Culture mindset and that starts with truly changing our perception of the physical building and embracing the revelation that we are the building.

Simon Says Worship

Simon says clap your hands, Simon says speak in tongues, Simon says shout to the top of your lungs. Simon says is the "do as I say," programmatic, habitual way of forcing people to meet our expectation of praising God the way we think is needed in the moment. Kingdom Culture is a culture of self-governance where there is no coercing needed to praise. Simon says is not referring to moments when the praise & worship leader is teaching and deliberately walking the congregation through any of the 7 levels of Praise. Training is necessary. However, in many cases we have traded modeling and leadership for coercing. The persona of God & Jesus has never been one of overriding a person's will in order to force an action. Jesus said "Behold I stand at the door and knock, if any man hears my voice and let me in, I will come in and sup with him and he with me." He didn't say he kicked in the door, made himself a plate and sat down. He knocked and waited for a response. In other cases, we see Jesus asking individuals if they wanted to be healed, giving individuals an option to follow him, and asking disciples if they're going to leave or stay.

Seeking to model after this is also the style and culture we as church leadership and leadership in general should take on. God does not want forced service. Since God does not require this from us, why do us Pastors and Leaders feel the need to force something "for God?" Are we forcing a response, forcing applause, a yell or a dance for our own affirmation? Do we not feel validated when we don't hear these responses? The need for validation is something we all have and it's important that we have this need for validation fulfillled. However, we must settle in our mind, soul and spirit that we are validated by God before we ever get in front of anyone else. Meditate on that and let it sink in daily.

Depending on life experiences, some people need more validation than others. For example, if you never had a father or mother to say "Son or daughter, I'm proud of you, you're doing a good job," perhaps your love bucket may need an extra gallon of validation, and that's okay. But if that place in you remains unhealed, you will transfer that need onto the church you're in a position to lead. There are many other areas where we transfer that need other than church—we transfer it to a spouse, siblings, family, and friends or from your profession. Those are big shoes for them to fill alone because you are expecting them to make up for what you didn't get in the past, provide for the present and future. Yes, God will use these individuals to validate you but one group or person alone should not be expected to bear the full weight of this need. Get a spiritual Father or Mother that can speak words of blessing over you and help instill the confidence you need. Get with God in a very personal connection through prayer and meditation so He can ultimately fill your need for validation and watch your confidence soar! No matter your narrative, God has validated you.

Their response is not correlated to your validation, get used to not needing to hear the "shout you down" yells of exuberant agreement. It will likely not be happening as much, because as you speak, the truth that deals in the area of needing to cut, dismantle, deconstruct, challenge and uproot this doesn't feel good and people aren't always going to "shout you down." When I go to my doctor, I'm not always shouting exuberant praises of agreement when he or she is either hurting me or telling me news I didn't want to hear. He's still doing a good job though because ultimately he is hurting me to help me! Pastor and Leader, even without all the exuberant praises of validation, you're still doing an excellent job! Keep Going!

No More Asking Permission

It is time for the body of Christ to stop asking permission. Disruptors don't ask permission. Jesus says that, "I only do what I see the Father doing." "I only say what I hear the Father saying." That was all the permission he needed—God's Permission! Why do congregants of many churches need permission from their Pastors and Leaders to engage in ministry assignments which God and Jesus have already commissioned them to do? Members have to ask permission or feel the need to ask permission for things they are already mandated to do through the word of God and by just being a believer.

For example, is it necessary to ask your Pastor to pray or prophesy to someone? No. The scripture tells you to pray without ceasing and scripture says I would that you all prophesy. Praying & Prophesying is a prerequisite for being a believer. Imagine it this way: when you start a new job, the first thing the employer does is give you a warm welcome and then off to orientation you go to receive the basic credentials you need to successfully operate in your new role. At orientation, one of the first things you get is a badge. Badges are much more sophisticated now. There was a time when all a badge would have is your name, the name of the company, your picture and a date. Now badges include that information plus a chip, similar to the chip found on your debit card. This chip contains your PII (personal identifiable information). With this upgrade came new functions for the user. You can scan it in once you enter and exit the building—this lets facilities management know exactly who is in the building at all times. It is also proof of you "clocking in" if you work on-site. But most importantly, now you actually use your badge to log into your workstation. There is a space on the computer to insert your badge, the computer reads that it's you and you log in to complete the work that you have been hired to do. After having gone through orientation—not even training yet—what if every morning when you got in to work, you went over to your Supervisor and said "is it okay if I use my badge to log in and complete my assignment?" My supervisor would think I was crazy! Of course use your badge to log in and work! There is no need to ask that question. I am already expected to use it.

After you have come into relationship with God through Jesus, you are saved or born again; Prayer and Prophecy are like the badge given at orientation. You don't have to ask to use it, you are expected to use it. Everything hinges on you using it. You have authority, and you are equipped at orientation alone. Some people will argue that you need training before you pray and training before you prophecy. Training is great and it will help you develop, become more knowledgeable and effective, but what you have is enough to get started. For example, consider if God got you off drugs and now you have confessed Christ and walk uprightly. Of course if you see someone going through what God had just delivered you from, you want to pray and prophesy over that person. At this point, you may not know all the types of prophecy but you can certainly use the creative style prophecy of Ezekiel 37 to your advantage. You speak to these dry bones and you command them to live! You encourage them in the same power that God used to deliver you from it.

As Church Leaders we have said in times past that we don't want any "water cooler prophets" or "parking lot prophesying," that everything said must be submitted to the Pastor or leadership for approval or that any prophecy given must happen in the main sanctuary so it can be supervised. We generally promote these ideas out of wanting to protect people from those with malicious intent, or any who don't have the spirit. However, I think it is time to reassess our methodology with this." Are these directives prohibiting the free move of the spirit more than they are promoting? Though I understand and commend leaders whose intent is to protect the people, I believe the current method is working against the very people we have trained and trust.

Most times there are only a very small few who have ill intent, can't be trusted or don't have the spirit. I don't want to punish an entire group of people I trust for a few that I don't. In most cases, reports will come back about the few we don't trust. Let's confront those individuals directly and mediate the situation. We don't want to punish the entire group because we are reluctant to confront specific individuals to whom it applies. We want water cooler prophets, parking lot prophets, and street prophets because everyone should be prophesying. The truth is, Kingdom Culture prophesying looks more like the water cooler and the parking lot. Think back on the woman at the well. Some of Jesus' best prophecy was at a water cooler. The woman went and won her entire city! She said "come hear the man who told me about my whole life." Most importantly, I want the church to get used to prophesying more "out there" without all the filters from church leadership in the sanctuary. This is what maturity and Kingdom Culture looks like. It is the sick who need a doctor, not those who are healed. It's the sick who need you, your encouragement, edification and comfort of your prophecy, not those who are already whole.

The next common permission seeking assignment is when a believer wants to conduct a home-based–or anywhere other than church building–bible study. In many places you have to get permission. Of course, it is wise and I do encourage you to share things like this with your Pastor, and the church for support, prayer support and because you are friends. But being expected to ask permission or get clearance is totally different and has no biblical basis but just a man-made preference. Matthew 28: 18-20 "Jesus tells His disciples to Go therefore, and make disciples of all nations, baptizing them in the name of the Father, Son and Holy Spirit, teaching them to observe everything I have commanded you. And remember, I am with you always, to the end of age. We know this to be the Great Commission, but not just a great commission to only the 12 Disciples but for all those like you and me who would come after them." We have been mandated by Jesus to preach, teach, baptize, counsel and use our authority through Him. An ordination and license through Pastoral Leadership is icing on the cake, but you do not need to wait on that to begin doing what Jesus already authorized and commanded you to do. You have been licensed by God to preach and teach. You don't need a microphone, pulpit, a Sunday or Wednesday night to do that. Wherever and whenever there are hurting people, that is your stage. Do what you do!

In times past, it has been practiced within many churches that we only allow a few select people to prophecy or preach. When I was coming up, it seemed as though prophecy was reserved for those who were older. I believe there was an authentic move of God in the place we were and a great church but maybe needed wisdom on what to do when a kid or young adult got the inspiration to prophecy. Kids and young adults were shunned from prophesying and other charismatic uses of the gifts but were primarily allowed to participate by giving a speech on "Youth Sunday" and "Easter Sunday" or performing a Christmas play. All this is great, but keep in mind that the youth are capable of more. I remember how people would get up and prophecy at my church, and one time, a cousin of mine who was a young boy got up in service and began prophesying to the congregation. He was immediately escorted out in the middle of the word being given and told he was acting "out of order." When it happened I felt ashamed and angry that he was treated that way. Why was it so far-fetched to them that a kid could prophesy? After all, the word says that God would be pouring out his spirit upon all flesh. Another example is when Saul just being in the company of prophets he also began to prophesy. Prophetic culture is so strong that you don't even have to be a "prophet" to prophesy—all you need to do is be in the atmosphere and your faith can be activated. During the few words my cousin was able to release, he mentioned a great ice storm in Atlanta. I'll have you know that this ice storm did come to pass. The word says you know if a prophet is true or false by whether or not their words come to pass. Kids and Young Adults are not only subject to activation on Youth Sunday—this is another on the "do not pack" list. We should be seeking ways to stir, develop and deploy their gifts of prophecy, intercession & works of ministry during general times when we gather.

The first thing we as believers must understand is that our badge of Prayer and Prophecy works not just in the church building; it works to influence the everyday life of the cultures in which we operate. Much of your discouragement is because you think the "church service" is your primary outlet for your anointing. However, I'm here to tell you that the church services on Sunday and Wednesday are not the primary outlet for your anointing and gifts. It is wherever the spirit leads and whatever cultures of influence you are anointed and gifted to influence.

Permission To Do It Differently

God has already given us, the body of Christ and all other cultures of influence the permission to do things differently. If you want to make an impact on this world and in your sphere of influence, it is going to be of utmost importance that you seek ways to do it differently. "Seek ways!" Research ways! And most importantly, ask the Holy Spirit for ways to do it differently. We don't want different just for the sake of being different. Many people have lost their passion and zeal because they constantly do things the same way year after year, generation after generation. I have personally experienced what it feels like to lose enthusiasm from too much of the same. The church is not the only place where this happens, it could be a marriage, a friendship, business or an event.

Passing The Juxtaposition Test

If I juxtapose you, it's because I value you. We live in a time where almost any disagreement with a person is perceived as "you hating." Like many things, this starts in the home. In some homes you really can't have a healthy dialogue where you can openly share your opposing views without being ganged up on and shamed all because you like something different, dismissed by phrases like "I'm the Mama," "I'm the daddy," "do what I tell you!" Then it continues when you join church family. The culture in many and I dare say most churches is that you never question or disagree with the Pastor and Leadership. If you do, then most will treat you as if something is wrong with you. Because this culture is so prevalent, Pastors then begin to feel like they can never be engaged on that level.

Every five-fold ministry gift should be welcoming people to engage, to dialogue and even if it's a different idea or opinion, but we're too worried about being "disrespected." Then we wonder why people are walking in timidity? This comes from years of feeling the need to repress what they really feel and think in the home and the church. But where is this scriptural? The Word says to judge and weigh every prophecy. Jesus said "let the little children come unto me." He had to juxtapose his own disciples on a few occasions, but they still loved each other. Apostle Paul traveled far, evangelizing and engaging people, welcoming them to oppose, dialogue, hear the truth and ultimately win over those whose hearts were ready.

Iron sharpening iron isn't someone always agreeing with you. There's going to be some friction and disagreement. Healthy conflict & relationships can be turned into toxicity when this is not understood. Regardless of differences in opinion, ideology or methods of doing things, we must always honor each other. If the church you're joined to has a set way of having prophecy heard by the Pastor or leadership before it's released, you should honor that. You can disagree with something and still show honor. It is not wise to leave a place of assignment at the first sign of disagreement. It is best to first determine what type of disagreement it is. Is it disagreement to sharpen you or the type of disagreement that stagnates your mission? Disagreement to sharpen you will usually be limited to about one or two things you disagree on, found in the word as an example and something that you know deep down will eventually help you but you are wrestling to be disciplined in an area. The word says wounds from a friend can be trusted; this is someone who has your best interest in mind and will disagree with you to help you. Disagreement to stagnate you is usually differing perspectives on many things and especially core values. This type of disagreement normally has no scriptural backing but stems from selfish motives of one or both of the parties. Jesus told his disciples how to handle disagreement that stagnates the mission. He said if you go to a town and they don't welcome you or heed your words, shake the dust off your feet. According to Benson's commentary, The Jews thought the land of Israel so peculiarly holy, that when they came home from any paganistic god loving country they stopped at the borders, and shook or wiped off the dust of it from their feet, that the holy land might not be polluted with it. Therefore the action here enjoined was a lively intimation, that those Jews who had rejected the gospel were holy no longer, but were on a level with pagans and idolaters. Another meaning is to simply move on and don't take the disappointment and rejection with you; leave it where it was. This is why honor is so important. If there are questions or opposing views on the way things are done you should speak with your Pastor or Leadership. Speak the truth in love and make sure you are willing to be the solution or at least have a solution.

Chapter 4: How Do We Reconcile Church Culture & Kingdom Culture?

Mouth to Mouth Resuscitation

When Elisha reached the house, there was a boy lying dead on his couch. He went in, shut the door and prayed to the Lord. Then he got on the bed and lay on the boy, mouth to mouth, eyes to eyes, hands to hands. As he stretched himself out on him, the boy's body grew warm. Elisha turned away and walked back and forth in the room and then got on the bed and stretched out on him once more. The boy sneezed seven times and opened his eyes (2 Kings 4: 8-36).

What places in your life have become dead, stagnant and seemingly irreparable? Are there any places in your life where the devastation of hurt and disappointment still linger? I have experienced some of these dark places in my own life. I needed help and continue to need it, but I do know that my life and my help are always present, just as yours are always present. All we have to do is ask.

I pray that the Holy Spirit of God will visit you mouth to mouth, eyes to eyes, hands to hands, and breathe new life into you. Church Culture and Kingdom Culture will be reconciled when the Kingdom of God stretches out over our half-dead Church Culture, mouth to mouth, eyes to eyes and hands to hands, healing our mind, soul, spirit and body. God breathe a vision into the church that propels us into complete alignment setting us on a course to complete fulfillment of your purpose & assignment. May the warmth of His comforting presence bring your spirit to say My Father Loves Me, now I will remain in His love, becoming one with Him?

Revelations 3:1-3

These are the words of him who holds the seven spirits of God and the seven stars. I know your deeds; you have a reputation of being alive, but you are dead. Wake up! Strengthen what remains and is about to die, for I have found your deeds unfinished in the sight of my God. Remember, therefore, what you have received and heard; hold it fast, and repent. But if you do not wake up, I will come like a thief, and you will not know at what time I will come to you.

Looking at the scriptures above, let's talk about the prophetic and symbolic meaning of numbers. For example, why did it highlight that the boy sneezed seven times and then opened his eyes? 7 is symbolic of the number of divine revolutions and cycles. It is the number of perfection and completion. There are 7 Days in a week—work 6 days, but on the 7th- Sabbath day, you rest. God created heaven and in earth in seven days, said it was good and rested on the seventh day. The boy Elisha stretched out over sneezed 7 times as he was brought back to life. This represented a completion in his life. The boy went from life to death and then back to life. This was symbolic of how Christ would later be born, die and be resurrected back to life by the power of the Spirit. When I see Elisha stretched out over the boy, I can imagine Father God stretched out over Jesus after His last breath on the cross, and bringing life back to Him in His resurrection. Then I imagine Jesus, at the same time, stretched out over the church and each of us to bring life back to us, never afraid to come and meet us exactly where we are. While we were yet sinners, Christ died for us. The same spirit that raised Christ from the dead now dwells in us. When the boy sneezed 7 times it was symbolic of the spirit of God breathing resurrection life to the seven churches, the seven continents of the world- (every people group), and all seven days of our weekly experience. Just as new life came when Elisha stretched out over the boy in complete alignment, this shows us as the church new life comes when we come into complete alignment with God and His Spirit. There is a great teaching by Jonathan and Amanda Ferguson where they teach three vital ways to align ourselves with the spirit:

1.) Being filled with the spirit (Ephesians 5:18).

2.) Being led by the spirit (Romans 8:14).

3.) Walking in the spirit. (Galatians 5:16).

As the Word has said in Revelations, we have a reputation of being alive, but we are dead spiritually. What it means is instead of being filled with the spirit, led by the spirit and walking in the spirit we are: filled with our own thoughts and desires, led by tradition and emotion, and walking by what we see. But now is the time for us to live again, but this time a "New Birth" where we are born of the spirit. Behold, He comes to make all things new. It is time for us to awaken! It is time for the church to awaken. It is time for the bride of Christ to remove every spot, blemish or wrinkle. One spot, blemish or wrinkle represents division and disunity within the bride. Christ is returning for "One" bride, which means the church has to be one (John 17). Christ is coming back for a church without a spot, blemish or wrinkle. Did you know that by preaching the gospel, completing your assignments, living holy, training your children, healing your family that you are preparing the bride? You are preparing the bride for His return.

What is one of the things that divide us? Denomination. Why is there a need for it? I find in scripture that Jesus came preaching a Kingdom message, not a denominational message. The church should dissolve all denominations. Jesus says we are one church. The focus should be on the Kingdom of God, and becoming one, not our differences. In fact, if we're all born of the spirit, believe in Christ and practice the principles He set forth. There is no difference; we are one body. We Can! Christ has already prayed for us to do just that and we will!

The Power of One

All throughout scripture the message of unity, becoming one and "the power of one" is very prevalent. God boldly declared that Jesus was His beloved Son with whom He was well pleased. In I John 2, the scripture goes into more declaration of that unity. It also mentions it again in John 17:23- I in them and you in me so that they may be brought to complete unity. Then the world will know that you sent me and have loved them even as you have loved me. Ephesians 5:25 says Husbands, love your wives as Christ loved the church. Christ loved the church so much He gave his own life for her. Christ views Himself as being one with the church. How do we know? One day Paul was on his way to beat and possibly kill more who belonged to "The Way" (the church), when suddenly a light shined from heaven and he heard a voice say to him, "Saul, Saul why are you persecuting me?" Paul says, "Who are you Lord?" He replies, "I am Jesus, whom you are persecuting." What amazes me is not only how Jesus declares His affectionate allegiance to us, but His oneness with us, to completely identify with us. Now is the time for us to completely identify with Him so we can walk in more success and use the keys He has given us. This is the year for us to become One with Him, One with His purpose in our lives, One with His identity for us as Kingdom citizens and heirs, One with the Holy Spirit, One with our brothers and sisters so that with one heart and one mind, we can glorify the God and Father of our Lord Jesus Christ. So today, let's aggressively pursue economic recovery, healing in families, in marriages and oneness with God.

A Return To Community

As I mentioned earlier, the early church had much more community as a church. They ate with each other house to house as they studied and fellowshipped around the word and daily living. Most of the times we see each other are at the appointed times for church gatherings. We rarely fellowship with each other outside of a "church event." This is not building relationships or friendships. Discipleship works best when there is relationship. By sticking to our routine of "going to church," focusing only on the duties of the church meeting and not the community, we are missing out on three vital things that are the lifeblood of any church or organization: Relationship, Friendship and Discipleship.

During my time as Pastor of Operations at Embassy International Worship Center in Atlanta, Ga., my role was to Pastor the sector leader of each ministry team. I really loved the team I had the privilege of leading. They are some of the best leaders I've ever met. One of the things I like to do as a leader to train and develop a team is to make book assignments, and in some cases review them together. One of the books I assigned was *The Secret of Teams* by Mark Miller. This book was a case study on what it takes to build "high performance" teams. They interviewed 10 of the most successful teams across different spheres of influence. The outcome of their study found that every "high performance" team possesses four attributes: Leadership, Skills, Talent and Community. Leadership is the overall vision, goals and direction. Skills dealt with competency, knowledge, ability especially after being trained. Talent was a natural ability to achieve. It was a person with character, competency and someone you have chemistry with. Community was known as the spirit of the team, camaraderie, relationship, friendship, genuine care and concern. So I thought it would be a great idea that since the book came with a survey that we complete it as a team and discuss it. The purpose of the survey was to see where we ranked as a team within the four areas of Leadership, Skills, Talent and Community.

The overall results of the survey found that we ranked high in Leadership, Skills and Talent but lower in the area of Community. Despite this, we still scored high enough in the area of community and were a high performance team. We continually improved in the area of community and accomplished some phenomenal things for God. But what the survey indicated is that in addition to coming together to sing praises, pray together and do ministry, we must invest more time and energy in cultivating healthy friendships with one another. Just as we had to address this on our teams, the church at large will need to improve community inside and out in order to reconcile with Kingdom Culture.

Jesus told Zacchaeus, "I must come to your house today." This is intentional relationship building that will later lead to discipleship. He didn't say, "Zacchaeus you gotta come visit my church, man." Jesus was the embodiment of the church and the Kingdom, which is exactly what we are when we abide in Him. If Jesus, the Word made flesh, the embodiment of the church and the Kingdom, is at Zacchaeus' home, anything is possible in Zacchaeus' home—healing, Special Miracles, generational curses broken—all over dinner.

Churches, Organizations, Marriages and Families go through this alike. We come together to complete the mission, but I don't know what your favorite food is, where you grew up, your story, what you're passionate about, what makes you happy, angry, what makes you laugh. In a marriage it looks like this: we come together to raise and talk about the kids but neglect to continue building the relationship with each other. This causes couples to become strangers in their own home and all they now have in common are the kids. New life is being breathed into defunct marriages & relationships. We must return to community, dwell with our spouses according to knowledge and know those who labor among us. This principle can be used more generally—Spend time with each other outside of the mission and ministry, go to lunch, dinner, do something fun, take trips, laugh and do life together.

A Self-Governing Kingdom

Matthew 25: 1-13 – At that time the Kingdom of heaven will be like ten virgins who took their lamps and went out to meet the bridegroom. Five of them were foolish and five were wise. The foolish ones took their lamps but did not take any oil with them. The wise ones, however, took oil in jars along with their lamps. The bridegroom took a long time coming, and they all became drowsy and fell asleep. At midnight the cry rang out: Here's the bridegroom! Come out to meet him! Then all the virgins woke up and trimmed their lamps. The foolish ones said to the wise, "give us some of your oil; our lamps are going out." "No, they replied, there may not be enough for both of us and you. Instead, go to those who sell oil and buy some for yourselves." But while they were on their way to buy the oil, the bridegroom arrived. The virgins who were ready went in with him to the wedding banquet. And the door was shut.

Later the others also came. "Lord, Lord," they said, "Open the door for us!"

But he replied, "Truly I tell you, I don't know you." Therefore keep watch, because you do not know the day or the hour.

First off, if I was going to preach a message after reading this, the title would be "I brought my own oil!"

The Kingdom of God is a self-governing Kingdom. The ten virgins who were prepared had to govern themselves. They didn't have the luxury to be reminded, prompted, pumped or primed to truly worship God. Let's talk about this oil. Think on other places in scripture and in nature on how oil is really given I can't recall a time it was given cheaply or without sacrifice. In nature, oil is produced from dead sea animals that decompose beneath the ocean's floor. In one part of scripture, oil was given to the widow woman of Zarephath in supernatural supply because she was sacrificial, humble and had faith enough to make Elijah a piece of bread first even though she was on her last and preparing to die. When David is anointed King of Israel, we see the oil poured onto his head by the prophet after 7 prior attempts of David's brothers. Oil costs! David was in the back, overlooked and rejected but still praising and worshipping, storing up oil for the journey God was about to take him on. If the Kingdom works in a reciprocal way, on earth as it is heaven, then the oil broke over David's head because David had stored oil throughout his life and sought after God with all of his heart. Therefore, heaven agreed with earth, and in that moment, the oil broke over his head. Oil is also produced through the pressing of olives. This pressing required much pressure, preparation and innovation. Knowing the investment, how costly and precious oil is, I find it interesting how the prepared virgins suggested that the unprepared virgins go buy them some last minute oil. I don't know about you, but I can't just run to the dollar store and buy oil for my destiny & purpose. Real Oil comes at a price and has to be prepared for. This reminds me of when the Israelites put the Ark on a new cart instead of carrying it on their shoulders. Here's that principle again! In the Kingdom of God, the method is just as important as the objective. I just can't go get this type of oil from the dollar store, it costs me something. It costs me sweat, tears, pain, some late nights praying, sacrificing what "I" wanted to do, and renewing my mind. With this in view, I can see how the unprepared five virgins were left behind. Based on the consequences of their slothful, unpreparedness and entitlement mindset, we see that all 10 of them were expected to govern themselves. They were to properly manage their time, efforts and energy with the goal of being fruitful and ready when it was their time to produce.

When you come with your own oil, you don't need anyone to pump, prime, yell and scream for you to praise the Lord. Pastors, Praise and Worship Leaders, Ministers—we all have to lead with this parable in perspective. Let's not disciple people into dependency by forcing them to praise. You be the praise and bring the oil you have stored up with anticipation of God showing up, and if you are only focused on Jesus, people will follow. The parable does not show the five unprepared virgins being pumped, primed or browbeaten to have their oil. No, they were expected to be ready and prepared to meet with Jesus. Have the same expectation when it is your time to lead them and watch how it boosts their faith and changes the atmosphere. Everyone has their own oil to bring, and not everyone has the same expression of praise. If we are to truly move into the Self Governing realm where we belong, we must give liberty to the people to praise and worship as they are led as well. This may be hard at first because the tendency to resort to the familiar or to perform has to be broken. It is that part of you that does it because it's what you know. But God wants you to be comfortable in the unfamiliar. If there is a moment where He is speaking to hearts and singing over His people, it's okay to fall back. Most of those moments I see a "ramp up" because "the quiet" and "the still" feels uncomfortable. God is in the loud Hala, Shabach and the quiet and still moments. We navigate them all just as a skilled singer goes from chest voice to head voice.

If the five virgins lived in our time now, they would not be the type of people who need someone to spoon feed them the how, what, where and when and how to praise their God. They wouldn't need to be reminded to stay in relationship with God. They would be the most disciplined masters of time and resources we have ever seen. They would not need anyone to tell them when to prophecy, when to pray for someone. They are about their business. On time for work, and taking care of their responsibility. They are like the ant storing up food daily and not waiting for one big moment to get started. They do little by little, day by day. They would definitely be tithers, but most of all they would have a life-giving relationship with God through Jesus Christ.

Uber, Airbnb & Lyft

Like never before we see this Kingdom Principle of Self-Governance being utilized and dominating in the culture of Business as it has catapulted them into multi-billion dollar companies while producing hundreds of thousands of jobs and millions of revenue streams for smaller businesses. There are three that I want to mention who had the innovation to implement this principle: Uber, Airbnb & Lyft. Uber and Lyft do not own the cars but they provide millions of rides to passengers. Airbnb doesn't own houses, but they provide shelter for millions of people around the world. The lynchpin of their business is that they trust people to self-govern. You can log into Uber or Lyft and drive as much as you want and log off when you're done. The owner of the car is responsible for their own car maintenance and upkeep. The owner of the car is responsible for keeping their registration, license and insurance updated on the app. With Airbnb, the owner is responsible for ensuring the home is clean before and after each resident uses it. They incentivize people by paying a fair wage and having a daily cash out option. There is no obligation or contracts that impede on their ability to self-govern and they can decide to stop whenever they're ready. Uber, Lyft and Airbnb are not forcing or coercing their users to do anything. They're simply providing an opportunity.

Different cultures of influence use Kingdom principles knowingly or unknowingly from the scripture and traveling light speed ahead while the church is either reluctant or slow in implementing them. The church is not in competition with other cultures, but should be open to see and learn from what God is doing in other areas and vice versa. The implementation of this principle alone mobilizes people to use what they have, and this is why I want people to have home-based, work or school empowerment groups where they study, worship, create, preach and teach. Our homes, cars, water coolers and parking lots should be hubs for Kingdom activity. All UBER and LYFT require is that your car not be older than a certain year and works properly. In the church, as long as you have the spirit and your revelation is current, go for it! Wherever you feel the urge to operate in your gift, turn it on and go! Even when you don't feel it, go anyway. There are so many times where I felt a power rising in me to act, but I either talked myself out of it or made an excuse for fear of confrontation. I now accept the call to confrontation. Renaissance and Revival happens where Confrontation Meets Competent Power." Competent Power is power under control. Many people exude power but do so out of control. Power has to be controlled by the Holy Spirit which is evident when the fruit of the spirit are on display. This is why Paul says without love I am but brass and tinkling cymbals. If you're operating in power but have no love, you're out of control. We know that life and death are in the power of the tongue. The book of James goes on to say that the tongue is like the rudder of a ship that guides or steers the direction of the ship. Your words will ultimately guide your life. They are very powerful and they especially need to be under the control of the spirit. According to Galatians 5:22-23 the fruit of the spirit is:

- **Love**
- **Joy**
- **Peace**
- **Patience**
- **Kindness**
- **Goodness**
- **Faithfulness**
- **Gentleness**
- **Self Control**

Operating with "Competent Power" will require you to ask the spirit how to respond, what to say and what to do. The next time you have a confrontation, right there in the moment, ask yourself: is there Competent Power for this problem? The answer is yes, the competent power resides in you. The same spirit that raised Christ from the dead now dwells in your mortal body. If you can't answer that question, just take a quick moment to ask the Lord to come into your heart, forgive you of your sins and believe in God through Jesus Christ and you can now say "Yes! That competent power to confront any situation now dwells in me." Where would the church be now if we were to embrace and implement all the kingdom principles available to us? I'm certain we would see more transformation in our cities and every culture of influence turned upside down. Let's accelerate our implementation of Kingdom Principles. Renaissance and Revival will happen at the speed of our implementation of Kingdom Principles.

Harness The Wind

I recently watched a phenomenal movie on Netflix that was based on a true story "The Boy Who Harnessed The Wind." Since you may want to view it I won't give any details and spoil it for you. As you may know, wind can be harnessed for energy, called "Wind Power." Wind is also symbolic of the spirit. There is the word Ruach- meaning wind or breath of God. During creation, God breathed into man the breath of life. The scripture also says that the spirit of God is like the wind. It is time for God's people to harness the wind that is blowing in our lives. In order to harness the wind, let us examine and utilize the technology of a windmill. I want you to see this in the spirit, our **relationship** with God, **prayers** and **obedience** to God—all of these represent a turbinate on the windmill. Once the spirit blows, the windmill begins to turn and power is created. **There are two primary types of windmills; one directional and omni-directional.** The one originally created was the one directional standard windmill which looks similar to a fan. The standard windmill has to be positioned in a certain place at the correct height and position to catch the wind. The influence of this windmill is generally localized to one place and culture. The other type is called the omni-directional windmill. With the omni-directional windmill, the turbines are contoured to catch the wind from any direction and produce power. This windmill has influence in all 7 cultures of influence and is like the wind power described in John 3:8- The wind blows wherever it pleases. You hear its sound, but you cannot tell where it comes from or where it is going. So it is with everyone born of the spirit. The one directional windmill is like your Salvation experience. It is effective and it is necessary. Jesus says no one can "see" the Kingdom unless they are born again. The one directional windmill is like the moment you are born again and can see the Kingdom. Then Jesus goes further to tell Nicodemus that no one can enter the Kingdom unless they are born of water and the spirit. The moment you enter the Kingdom is like an upgrade to the omni-directional windmill where you have been born of water and the spirit and are thrust further into your assignment. We must first see the Kingdom and then enter the Kingdom. You have a one directional windmill and then you get an omni-directional windmill. God has already prophesied upgrade when He said in the last days, He would be pouring out His spirit upon all flesh (Acts 2:17). God wants many of us to upgrade. A one directional is not obsolete, it is necessary, you see and then enter. But many have gotten comfortable seeing and not entering. We can't get comfortable just seeing the Kingdom, we must enter it. We can't get comfortable looking at all the harvest in the fields, we must commit as laborers to enter it. The wind of God is blowing in many areas of our lives. Are our windmills erected and set in place to harness the power of the Holy Spirit? The wind blows through our families, our jobs, our churches, our Government, Our Businesses, culture, Education, Media, Religion, and Arts & Entertainment. Where are the windmills?

We have grace for a while to be recipients of the power generated from those in our lives– Parents, Pastors & mentors– who have established windmills to sustain our way of living and provide our basic needs. This is particularly important when we are young and do not have the knowledge and understanding to do it for ourselves. However, there is a coming of age in our lives where God expects maturity out of us. He expects us to have our own windmill constructed. This is the moment where you can no longer survive solely off of listening to the revelation and testimony of others. You can no longer rely on just the sermon from your Pastor or just the song from your praise team. God wants to blow revelation through your windmill, songs, creativity and innovation in your spirit. This does not mean we alienate our Parents, Pastors and mentors, but their role in our lives takes on a different function. When you have your own windmill, you are then able to strengthen them and synergize your wind with theirs to strengthen the broader culture of the Kingdom.

In church culture, we habitually attempt to harness the wind of another person or church. For example, when we gather the majority of songs we sing every week are from a small handful of artists or TOP 40 radio. Many churches are in awe of the windmill others have constructed and the potency of the songs being produced. There is nothing wrong with singing the songs of other congregations, but we are so enamored with it that it is causing us to neglect the windmill we should be constructing.

I live in Atlanta, if there is a windmill in Atlanta and a windmill in Australia, which windmill am I going to get more direct power from? The songs by the artists we love to sing along to are produced from their intimacy with God, their testimony and their dealings with God, and I believe the songs have a greater impact to strengthen and edify other souls right in the place their windmill is constructed. This is similar to how a Pastor or Shepherd feeds his own sheep—he knows what they need and what diet is necessary for their journey, so he leads them to those streams and pastures. Similarly, song creation and the leading of worship is more than just picking three songs from your favorite artist or constantly singing TOP 40 radio. Yes, we should incorporate songs from our favorite artists and radio songs, but it should not be a substitute for creating our own windmill. Sing unto the Lord a new song. When we meet, everyone has a song, hymn or spiritual songs.

It's time for churches and individuals to build their own windmill. There are songs that come from your people that have an assignment to directly edify your local church, spark deliverance, heal, and boost creativity and innovation, but we're rarely seeing them because many churches are not creating a windmill in their own house. Creating a windmill takes time, study, energy, it is a sacrifice—but it's fun and it's worth it! This act of creation is quality time spent with your team and friends to simply worship God together. Normally, it won't feel like work because each of you have a passion for God and the supernatural. It looks like an overflow of the move of God that even when the gathering ends, the presence of God still lingers and hearts are changed. It looks like your local church singing the songs that are created by individuals in your local church. It looks like creating songs that can be used outside of church gatherings as well: a mayoral campaign, movie, ad or sitcom score. It looks like incorporating the songs and spiritual songs into corporate worship gatherings and stop neglecting them. We have yet to see the untapped power than can hit our houses because we are neglecting the very power that is in our own houses. These songs contain the testimonies, the favor and goodness, the dealings of God specific to that assembly and that region; by and large it will have greater impact and influence in our churches than just hymn selections and TOP 40 radio. The power from your own windmill has the greatest impact on you first! Create your windmill and harness the wind!

Two types of windmills: one directional and omni-directional. (Creative illustration courtesy of Belinda Jackson for "Picture it Possible").

Push Away- Permission To Do It Differently

God has already given us the body of Christ and all other cultures of influence the permission to do things differently. If you want to make an impact on this world and in your sphere of influence, it is going to be of utmost importance that you seek ways to do it differently. "Seek Ways!" Research Ways and most importantly ask the Holy Spirit for ways to do it differently. We don't want different just for the sake of being different. Many people have lost their passion and zeal because of constantly doing things the same way year after year, generation after generation. I have personally experienced what it feels like to lose enthusiasm because of doing things the same way for too long. We often sing the same songs, watch people shout on que to the same inflection of a tone or word, pray for the same people at the altar for the same thing and go through the same motions.

The church is not the only group of people this happens to, it could be a marriage, family, a friendship, business or an event. One generation grows up in the ghetto then another and another. With generation to generation growing up in the ghetto, most will practice a ghetto culture and poverty mindset. Having lived in the Perry Homes projects in Atlanta, where I was probably first introduced to ramen noodles, I'm still trying to break the ghetto culture off me and my family. I finally stopped eating them but then I relapsed. But when I relapsed I got creative in order to feel better about it. So I would go to the store and buy four packs of ramen noodles and thin spaghetti noodles. I would cook the thin spaghetti noodles and only add the seasoning pack from the ramen noodles. By substituting the thin spaghetti for ramen noodles, I justified the relapse because it was a healthier option. I guess! But no, this wasn't right for me or my health so I have since finally stopped eating them for good! This is an example about food that shows us how strong culture is once it is ingrained and how it has to be dealt with. I know firsthand what it is to struggle with poverty, to see people I love struggle with alcoholism, drug addiction and selling drugs. I saw how drugs, crime, poverty and injustice affected my family, my city and how we are still making strides to rewrite previous chapters of history. We are in a battle to establish new culture.

There is a scripture that I want to highlight that really brings light to this area and shows us how to be different. In Luke 4:43 Jesus says "I must proclaim the good news about the Kingdom of God to the other towns also, because I was sent for this purpose." And He was preaching in the synagogues of Galilee. This lets us know a few things:

1.) The people of God who go to a building to worship or the "institutional church" are God's children whom He loves and He made it a priority to preach to them. "We can never throw the baby out with the bathwater." We need to preach the gospel to not only our churches where we belong but to churches in other cities. I'm speaking to the body of believers who are the "Organic Church," "New Testament Church" or anyone who has said "I'm done with church." Here is what I say: I'm not done with church, I'm done with empty religious church culture. I am done with everything that is not Gospel, Kingdom Culture or Kingdom Mindset in the church. I can still love the traditional, institutional church. I fellowship, preach the Kingdom there and minister, but choose not to adopt unfruitful methods or things I disagree with. If you can take on this mindset, God can use you anywhere, anytime, because this is exactly what He did with Jesus. But if you are bitter with the church, this is a blockage from you being a conduit for which He can flow and use your anointing to help the church. Imagine some of the children of Israel who were ready to go into the promised land on day number 11 but ended up having to wander 40 years around the same Mountains, through valleys and the deserts in the wilderness, all because the people they were associated with would rather have their culture than God's culture. Can you imagine their level of bitterness and anger toward the rest of the family? This is 40 years of my life—trapped and wandering. But they still had to forgive. You need to forgive the church for the time you lost wandering mundane Mountains, for the missed opportunities because you were always "in church" being hurt, disappointed and even rejected. Give all of that to God and in return, receive His love, acceptance and know that He is going to restore to you double what you lost!

2.) In Luke 5:1-4 As the crowd was pressing in on Jesus to hear God's word, He was standing by Lake Gennesaret. He saw two boats at the edge of the lake; the fisherman had left them and were washing their nets.

Let's break this down! First, the two boats at the edge of the lake have prophetic meaning. A boat is a mode of transportation, and modes of transportation for water are symbolic of flowing in your gifting, anointing, assignment, calling, spiritual movement and ability. They're at the edge of the lake. When I hear this I see a boat partially docked on land and the other part in the water. This represents one foot on land in Church Culture and one foot in water, Kingdom Culture. It's one foot in what's comfortable and familiar and the other foot in the unknown or supernatural.

When Jesus got to the disciples, they had already been fishing for a long time; they were out of the boats and washing their nets. Just by the mere fact that they were out of their boats and washing their nets meant they had given up. They were outside of their calling, and calling it quits on the promise. It didn't work. They had decided enough was enough. I'm done. I'm done with this marriage, done with this family, done with my calling, done with church, done with God, I did everything I could but the business still went under. Like the disciples, are you outside of the boat and washing your nets?

Then Jesus did something that only He can do. In verse 3, the bible says that Jesus got into one of the boats that belonged to Simon—in effect, Jesus gets into something that they've already given up on. If Jesus gets in the boat, if Jesus goes ahead of me and gets into my calling, my anointing, my assignment, my family, my marriage, my business, my ministry, it is sure to be resurrected; it has no choice but to get up because HE IS the resurrection! He then asked Simon to push out a little from the land. Push away from the safety of the shore of Church Culture where you preach in the same pulpit every week and fully immerse yourself into Kingdom Culture where I can use you anywhere, anytime to preach the gospel. Push away from the comfort of what is familiar. Then Jesus began teaching the crowds from the boat. Imagine Jesus getting in a boat, pushing out about 10 feet from land and teaching a crowd on land. How many would dare break protocol in this day to introduce something new? This is the epitome of what it looks like to implement new ways and not have to ask permission or second guess yourself. This is Kingdom Innovation!

After he finished speaking, he said to Simon, Put out into the deep water and let down your nets for a catch. Master, Simon replied we've worked all night long and caught nothing, but at your word, I'll let down the nets. Operating in church culture doing it our way will have us toiling, doing plenty of work with little to no results. So they have progressively gone from just a little way from the shore to now in deep water. This is a trifecta progression of Kingdom Cycles often seen in scripture:

- and/water, shallow water, deep water
- 30, 60, 100 fold
- ankle deep, waist deep, swimming deep
- past, present and future
- one plants, one waters, GOD gives the increase
- Righteousness, Peace and Joy

These are all free flowing systems that we will explicitly delineate in a later book titled "Kingdom Cycles." Now we have gone from washing our nets, having given up, to pushing away to deep waters with Jesus in the boat. In one account Jesus told them to let down their nets on the other side of the boat. Again, He shows us the power of trying something different. Same boat, but they let down the nets on the opposite side and pulled up so many fish that their nets began to break, the boat began to sink and they had to call for their partner boat to come help with the catch. Don't give up! Stop washing your nets! It ain't over! Jesus is in your boat—can you see Him? Push away and watch what happens!

Restoring The Joy Of Your Salvation

Create in me a clean heart O God and renew a right spirit within me. Cast me not away from thy presence and take not thy Holy Spirit away from me. Restore unto me the joy of thy salvation; and uphold me with thy free spirit. Then I will teach transgressors thy ways; and sinners shall be converted unto thee. Recently when I read this verse it hit me entirely different. This time I knew exactly what my problem had been over the last several years. I had lost the joy of my salvation. Though I still love God, still do ministry, still gather with the church, I was doing all of this without the joy of my Salvation. This totally explained why I stopped wanting to attend the local church gatherings, why I became critical of many things within the church and eventually why I wasn't praying and communing with God as I should have been. This also explains why I hadn't shared my faith passionately enough to cause sinners to believe. I stopped winning souls. It was amazing to me how this scripture in Psalm 51 says when we have the Joy of our Salvation, sinners are converted to God. So we know the converse has to be true, when we don't possess the joy of our Salvation, sinners are not converted.

Here are a few ways to know if you have lost the joy of your Salvation:

- No desire to attend church or attend occasionally
- Have left the church
- Still love God but have lost intimacy with God
- Still love God's people but disagree on how things are done.
- No Sinners Converted- i.e. No Evangelism
- Feel Isolated

Why is the joy of our Salvation diminished?

The Joy of Salvation is diminished in two ways:

Willful Sin- These are obvious sins that you engage in that you know are wrong and cause you to be more conscious of your sins than of God's grace and righteousness. It's a lack of faith in God. Not having the Word of God hidden in your heart and obeying its command. Normally after you sin you feel distant from God and his people. This can cause you to distance yourself from God and his church because of your own personal shame.

Empty Religion- Empty Religion is our way of doing things instead of God's way. It is empty religion that does not exhibit the fruit of the spirit. It is void of love. It's like the struggle of being unequally yoked. It is having a form of Godliness but denying the power thereof. It is based on performance, ritualistic tradition and not the grace of God. Has no control over the tongue. Does not look after orphans and widows in their distress and stained by the world. Empty Religion steals the joy of our Salvation. If empty religion is part of your church culture, get rid of it.

Once Willful Sin or empty religion is in operation, the Joy of our Salvation is diminished.

We must take back the word religion; it is not a bad word. The bible says there is a true religion. If there is "true religion there must be "false religion," and this is the same as empty religion.

What does true religion look like?

True Religion- True Religion is an existence in the Kingdom. It is Pure, experiences Righteous Peace and Joy in the Holy Ghost. Experienced with doing it God's way. It operates in love. It exhibits the fruit of the spirit. Has control of its tongue. Looks after orphans and widows in their distress and is unstained by the world. (James 1:27) It gives to those in need.

How do we recover the Joy of our Salvation?

In order to experience full joy you need to be resolved in the fact that you are righteous and you have peace with God. Without either of these two being complete in you, it is hard to experience the Joy of your Salvation.

Romans 14:17– For the **Kingdom of God is** not meat and drink; but **righteousness,** and **peace,** and **joy in the Holy Ghost.**

What's important to know is that everything Paul says leading up to verse 16 describes and dismantles the empty religious church culture that is holding them and others back from experiencing the Kingdom.

First it says to: Accept any who is weak in the faith. The first thing we like to do is debate trivial issues, impose our will on the people who are not as strong in the faith and indoctrinate them into "tradition" and our local "Church Culture." "The way we do it "around here is _____." But no, the bible says we are to accept them in the state they are in. They are not going to talk like you, act like you, dress like you or even agree with all the truth you may have knowledge of. Accept means to agree to receive and to welcome.

1.) Don't look down on or criticize those who don't believe the same on issues. God has already accepted them.

Coupled with how we defined it as earlier in the book, The Kingdom of God is also righteousness, peace and joy in the Holy Ghost. Let's take a deeper look at these.

Righteousness– from the word dikaiosyne- (dik-ah-yos-oo-nay) means: integrity, virtue, purity of life, rightness, correctness of thinking feeling and acting, condition acceptable to God, ***Being and feeling Approved of God.***

Peace- from the word eirene- (i-ray-nay) means: security, safety, prosperity, harmony, tranquil state of a soul assured of its Salvation through Christ. ***Being and feeling joined to God.***

Joy- chara- (khar-ah) means: cheerfulness, calm, delight, gladness, exceeding joyfulness. ***Being and feeling exceeding gladness and delight in God.***

Let's sum the three up this way:

Righteousness- *Being and feeling approved of God*

Peace- *Being and feeling joined to God*

Joy- *Being and feeling exceeding gladness and delight in God*

When you walk in the experience of his righteousness & peace your joy will be full. Please understand that just because you don't feel approved by God or joined to God doesn't mean it's true. Emotions and feelings are not always true. But emotions and feelings come from thoughts. What thoughts are you having that cause you not to feel approved of God or joined to him and why? Have you been burdened under the weight of a church culture that says you're not good enough unless you serve this much, praise this hard, pray this hard? If you have I know just how you feel because I have been there. Even though I have much love for them and they are great churches, I have experienced the feeling of not being approved by Pastoral Leadership or God if I did not or was not willing to serve hard enough in Leadership. In leadership we are told that we must sacrifice on a higher level. I learned and began to know instinctively this level of sacrifice is not even required by God. The church has gotten this way because we think it's about performance and not grace. I had to ask God recently, is there anywhere in my life where I'm trying to perform to be approved or feel joined to you? I recently heard a testimony on the Bishop's Village- (an online platform created by Bishop T.D. Jakes) from Pastor Keion Henderson. It moved me to tears to hear of the incredible pain he overcame! However, what impressed me the most was how honest and vulnerable he was in describing how he longed for a relationship with his Dad. Because of this longing unfulfilled it created a performance culture in his life. If I perform good enough maybe my dad will make me feel approved and joined. As a successful Pastor, Businessman, Husband & Father he deals with the nuisances of feeling the need to perform. Like Keion, many of us have similar backgrounds, but have we stopped long enough to ask the question and assess if the need to perform is inculcated into the fabric of our culture as well?

I spent some of my childhood in a single parent home as well and I definitely longed for a genuine relationship with my Father. Though we lived in the same city, our relationship was thousands of miles apart. Though my Mother and Father's marriage did not work out I still love both of them dearly. My Father is not a bad man just because their marriage didn't work. He has many good qualities that I see in me and know they came from him. He's also a joy to be around, very charismatic, a people person. My mother has so many great qualities that I inherited as well! She is an intercessor at heart and when she prays, things happen! One thing I wish were different is how much our relationship was impacted because of the condition of her marriage with my Father, it ending and her becoming the sole provider for the family. I think when this happened she took on a stronger personality (which was already strong) by default and we experienced a lot of friction. My relationships with both of my parents have improved over the years. One day when I was younger I went to my dad and told him how his absence made me feel, how rejected, hurt and disappointed I felt. He listened, he cried (maybe we both cried a little) and he said he was sorry but he thinks about us every day and that we can start from there on building a better relationship. For the young boy in me who longed just to play catch or see my dad in the stands at one of my basketball games, those words were very freeing for me and brought a level of healing that I really needed.

I realize this goes much deeper for some people—those who were made to feel as though they were not approved or joined if they did not give sexual gratification to that Pastor, Clergyman or Leader. Or, if you didn't give large sums of money or pretty much do anything else they said do. This was wrong and you should never have been violated by someone you trusted as a spiritual father or mother. The good news I have for you is that these things are not of God, nor required by Him, and God is freeing His people from the bondage of empty religious church culture and advancing us into the Kingdom! Righteousness, Peace, Joy in the Holy Ghost, Righteousness Peace and Joy in Holy Ghost, that's the Kingdom of God! Don't you wanna be a part of the Kingdom? C'mon everybody!

Where did we get the doctrine that everything has to be so intensely sacrificial, a hard grind and struggle to have Righteousness, Peace and Joy? Jesus says come to me all you who are heavy laden and I will give you rest. Take my yoke upon you, my yoke is easy and my burden is light. It is time for the people of God to give back the heavy yoke of church culture and take on the yoke of Christ.

Everything we get is by the grace of God, not through how hard you serve at church, how hard you sing praises, how much you yell, or how hard you pray. Or, are you just lacking in faith because of not embracing the truth of the word about you? I want you to remember these three things:

Righteousness- *Being and feeling approved by God*

Peace- *Being and feeling joined to God*

Joy- *Being and feeling exceeding gladness and delight in God*

Repeat this aloud: I am Righteous through Christ. I have Peace; I have the fullness of Joy! I am approved by God! I am joined to God! I am delighted in Him.

Chapter 5: The Law of Reciprocity

"The Law of Reciprocity" is defined as continual synchronous interactions that affect one another in the spiritual or natural world. Any time you talk about reciprocity it is in reference to something being given in exchange for something else given. Reciprocity is defined as the practice of exchanging things with others for mutual benefit, especially privileges granted by one country or organization to another. Jesus gave His life for me; therefore, I give him my life.

He gives me a car- I give rides to people who may not have a car. He gives me a house; I house people who don't have a home. He gives me time, favor & blessings; I share these with those who may not be favored or blessed. I choose to also hang with people of lower stature.

In order to sustain any ecosystem, the Law of Reciprocity has to be in operation. God created the heavens and the earth and enacted the Law of Reciprocity. The heavens and earth have been practicing the law of reciprocity every moment ever since. It has so many reciprocal relationships. For example: rain comes down, the earth gives up crops. If this stops even for a season, you lose everything you planted and were expecting as a harvest.

In creation, God created many systems of reciprocal interaction. Meaning they cannot function or operate without the reciprocal reaction from its counterpart. Example: the clouds give the earth rain, the earth give clouds humidity. Explain reciprocal interaction between the Atmosphere, Lithosphere, Hydrosphere and Biosphere. These systems were created one time, but through perpetual implementation of the Law of Reciprocity, they last a lifetime. This is a great model for our relationships with each other. The problem is we have too many takers: people who, take your money, take your energy, take your time and take your attention. They don't reciprocate, just take.

Reciprocal Authority

On earth as it is in heaven. Whatever we bind on earth shall be bound in heaven. Whatever we lose on earth shall be loosed in heaven. This is Reciprocal Authority.

How do we get authority? Just be a son or daughter. The first thing that comes to our mind is how we can get it through work? But true reciprocal authority isn't performance-based, it's heart-based and comes as a result of being a child of God.

Reciprocal Interaction

In creation, God created many systems of reciprocal interaction. Meaning they cannot function or operate without the reciprocal reaction from its counterpart. Example: the clouds give the earth rain, the earth give clouds humidity.

Our world is comprised of four different spheres that make up the earth and are in constant reciprocal interaction: Hydrosphere, Geosphere, Atmosphere and Biosphere.

Hydrosphere– Water: rivers, lakes, streams, glaciers, air moisture.

Geosphere– Ground and Land: minerals, rocks found in and on earth.

Atmosphere– Air: all of the planet's air.

Biosphere– Life: all living organisms on earth.

These systems were created one time but through perpetual implementation of the Law of Reciprocity, they last a lifetime. The four spheres are very closely connected. A change in one often results in a change in one or more of the other spheres. For example: if there is an oil spill out in the ocean- Hydrosphere, by contaminating the water it affects living animals and humans of the Biosphere who depend on clean drinking water and fish to eat. Eventually the contamination causes dead animals and fish to wash ashore and now it affects the Geosphere. An event is a change that takes place in one of the spheres. Events can occur naturally, by humans or by the effect of changes in other spheres. The two way cause and effect relationship between event and sphere is called an interaction. The Law of Reciprocity is a technology God uses to teach us of His abundant nature and to produce abundance in our lives. When we begin to utilize reciprocal interactions in our relationships and in our ministry, it is going to be powerful. When we begin to pinpoint the negative reciprocal interactions and replace those with Kingdom reciprocal interactions, we are going to be unstoppable.

```
                              |
                              |
                              |
         Hydrosphere        ←→        Atmosphere
                              |
  ──────────────────↕────────┼────────↕──────────────
                              |
         Geosphere          ←→        Biosphere
                              |
                              |
                              |
```

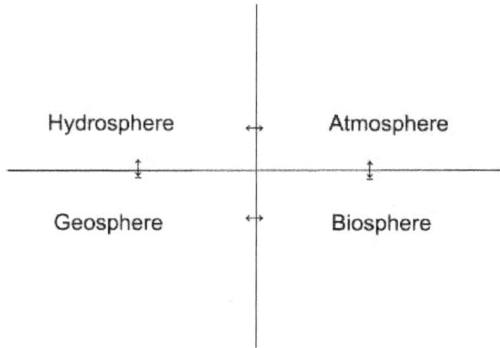

Selective Reciprocity

Selective Reciprocity is when you pick and choose to practice the law of reciprocity based on when it directly benefits you. An example of this is celebrity culture. The problem with some celebrity culture is that it operates against the law of reciprocity. The empty tradition of this culture teaches you to only reciprocate if the person has a certain socioeconomic status or only reciprocate if they have a certain amount of money, prestige, or followers. But the word tells us, how can you love me who you haven't seen and hate your brother who you have seen?

The climb to get to celebrity culture for some turns into clout chasing. Clout Chasing is when a person will compromise their character or do illegal stuff to acquire prestige, power or notoriety. This person is usually driven by a love for prestige, material possessions and upper echelon social status.

Creative Pressure

Creative pressure is the pressure that initiates reciprocity and is experienced during and as a result of creating. Every leader has the responsibility to be creative. In fact, every person "created" has the responsibility to be creative.

How did Jesus experience creative pressure? All pressure has to have an initiator. Other than being sent, I believe the initiator for Jesus was found in this statement: "I only do what I see the Father doing; I only say what I hear the Father saying." Can you imagine the pressure just from this statement alone? But I'm convinced and know without a shadow of a doubt that this was the lynchpin to Jesus' superhuman creative works while He was here in the earth. How did He have such a tremendous level of spiritual sight and hearing? It is because He always maintained a reciprocal interaction, a reciprocal love for Father God. Coming to earth and taking on an earthly body didn't cause Him to lose it. Ridicule, slander and mistreatment from people didn't cause him to lose it. Even death on a cross through crucifixion didn't cause Him to lose it. Truly nothing ever separated Him from the love of God. I want this to sink deep in your spirit, and for it to do so we have to establish one thing first: you are more spirit than you are physical body. Did you know you existed in the spirit long before you were sent here to earth? The word says He knew me from before my Mother's womb. From Before! You were already thought of, already planned for, full of purpose, full of anointing, full of gifting, with a blueprint of assignments. Would a God this loving send you to earth and not give you some instruction and guidance on your life? Absolutely Not! But what has been happening for most of your life is, you have probably identified with your human experience and concerned yourself mostly with human or physical things: where you will eat, sleep, work, what organization you will join. This is only one aspect of who you are. The more essential part of you that often goes ignored is your soul and spirit. This is the invisible you but is just as real as if you were to touch your nose right now. Do we ever stop to say what should my spirit eat today, what does my spirit eat, what does my spirit need, and what environment does my spirit thrive in? How is my soul doing? The soul houses your mind, will and emotions.

The soul and spirit are intermingled but different. God wants your soul and spirit to be not only made whole but to be led by His spirit. This has long been an impediment to us truly becoming like Christ in experiencing the level of intimacy He had to only do what He saw the Father doing. But now that we have established the extreme significance of the spiritual experience and the spirit you, you are about to experience another level of creative ability. God desires that we have this type of relationship with Him. This is why He showed us through Jesus.

Chapter 6: Consecration or Sequestration?

One day I was thinking about how I try to handle things on my own most of the time. It is rare that I ask for help even though I could really need it. Considering some of the circumstances surrounding how I grew up, I do understand why I behave that way. During some of my teenage years, my mom worked two jobs and I had to take care of my younger siblings. Then, I left home at 17 and went to live in Florida with a wonderful church family. I had to become responsible very quick, and this may be the case for many of you. In doing that, I made the mistake of becoming too self-reliant and grew silently frustrated when things got too hard or fell apart. This set of circumstances is the perfect mix for someone to be around people but still be sequestered. It's where you cut yourself off from people physically, emotionally and spiritually because you have become accustomed to handling things on your own. Somewhere in the mix of this is a lack of trust for people. Though it appears as a sequestration from people, it's really from God because God uses people. A few days ago I asked God why was I like this and then asked for His help. He reminded me of His word and said My name is a strong tower, the righteous run into it and are safe. "You have been relying on yourself too much." "Begin relying on Me." Now, I am rediscovering that scripture in Proverbs 18:10 and seeing it in a whole new light. There are many kinds of towers that serve different purposes. However, by definition a tower is a tall structure. They are built extremely firm and can sustain heavy turbulence. No matter your situation, the name of the Lord is a strong tower. Run into His name. His name is who He Is. He is Love and His love is expressed in many ways. He is what you need and far greater.

Consecration is set apart to be Holy. Sequestration is just set apart. One has a motive and purpose directly God centered while the other is set apart for other reasons maybe rejection, distrust for people, selfish ambition or pride. Consecration is set apart to be apart, while sequestration is set apart to look apart. Consecration says I'm only set apart to do the will of the Father while the other says I'm doing my own will. One furthers the cause of evangelism while the other is the reason Jesus said the laborers are few. Sequestration is satisfied with ordinary church attendance, programs and events. They usually believe no one does it better than them and it becomes the illusional error of their sequestration. No one does ministry like us. No one does business like us. We got it going on and no one else does. Churches, businesses and individuals who maintain this belief have bought into a lie and are as a result sequestered from those who can help them and those who they could be helping.

Do you remember when Elijah was under extreme pressure and thought he was the only one living Holy? He thought he was the only one living a consecrated life and because of this error he sequestered himself off. In this time of sequestration God reminded him that He had 7,000 more people living Holy and consecrated just like he was. Anytime you feel as though you're the only one doing it, or no one does it like you, just remember what God told Elijah—there are 7,000 more who are getting the job done. Many have been tempted to believe this, but the good news is that you can come back to the truth. I believe in many ways the church has wandered from consecration to sequestration, and this is not by chance. Many have done it through lack of understanding or misinterpretation of what it means. The powers and rulers of darkness have an agenda to sequester the church, make us isolated, irrelevant and hidden away. In a place of sequestration, our influence, effectiveness and reign will be diminished in the earth. This is not the will of the Father that our influence be diminished. He says who lights a candle and hides it under a bushel? The question now becomes, are you lit? I mean really lit? See, there is a tendency to sequester your gift or personality due to a lack of confidence. But your gift can't grow, develop or bless anyone if it remains sequestered. It is time for you to come out of sequestration. We are like a city on a hill that cannot be hidden.

2 Corinthians: tells us "be ye separate and touch not the unclean thing." This being separate here is describing our consecration not sequestration to the Lord. Holiness has been reduced to simply not fornicating, committing adultery and wearing modest clothes. We generally speak at length on what it isn't, but let's talk about what it is. Holiness and consecration are so much more. Dr. Matthew Stevenson has a phenomenal series entitled "Road To Romans" where he deals with this subject in great detail. Here is what Paul says about what it means to be Holy in Romans 12 and Colossians 3:

- Present bodies as a living sacrifice.
- Not conforming to this age (this world or culture).
- Be transformed by the renewing of your mind.
- Discern what is good, pleasing and perfect will of God.
- One Body- many parts and different functions. One body in Christ and individually members to one another.
- Prophecy according to the standard of faith.
- Serve according to faith.
- Teach according to faith.
- Exhort according to faith.
- Give with generosity.
- Lead with diligence.
- Show mercy, with cheerfulness.
- Love without hypocrisy.
- Detest evil.
- Cling to what is good.
- Show family affection to one another with brotherly love.
- Outdo one another in showing honor.

- Do not lack diligence, serve the Lord; be fervent in spirit; serve the Lord.
- Rejoice in hope, be patient in affliction, be persistent in prayer.
- Share with the saints in their needs, pursue hospitality.
- Bless those who persecute you; bless and do not curse.
- Rejoice with those who rejoice, weep with those who weep.
- Be in agreement with one another.
- Do not be proud, instead associate with the humble.
- Do not be wise in your own estimation.
- Do not repay anyone evil for evil.
- Try to do what is honorable in everyone's eyes.
- If possible, on your part, live at peace with everyone.
- Do not avenge yourselves; instead leave room for his wrath.
- Vengeance belongs to me, I will repay says the Lord. .

Holiness goes far beyond the few parameters that we grew accustomed to defining it as. As we see outlined from Romans 12 and Colossians 3, Holiness is an everyday lifestyle of grace in motion. Creative pressure is building within the church and the Kingdom and is about to push us from sequestration into consecration.

Chapter 7: Managing Your Kairos

Throughout my life I can remember specific times when God would insert a significant moment. These are moments when something happens to push me into my purpose and destiny. One of the most pivotal and significant moments came when I was attending Pebblebrook High school. The first two years I was an average student, pretty much doing enough to get by making average grades. During this time I had a love for basketball. I had been practicing all the time since I was a little boy, but for some reason I never made the team at Pebblebrook. I tried out freshman year, got cut; tried out sophomore year, got cut; and was ultimately told I needed to go to the summer basketball camp to heighten my chances of making the team. I went to the camp, but junior year I still got cut. Meanwhile at home it's very stressful; my parents got a divorce, so my Mom was taking care of me and three other siblings. My household was very strict—we had to be sneaky about listening to anything other than gospel.

One day my friend Richard asked me if I wanted to join ROTC. He was already a member and had always been a leader from a very young age. At this point I was tired of being an average student and I knew if I wanted any shot at going to college something had to change. So I joined ROTC my junior year and things immediately turned around for me. I became more disciplined as a student and my grades improved tremendously. I was now an honor roll student and also joined the Student Leadership Team that same year. During this time I was serving with a great church- Dominion World Outreach Center and we had guest Pastors David & Vernette Rosier from Florida come for a conference. At the end of the conference the Pastor walked up to me and told me about their church, in Panama City, Florida which also had a private school and invited me to attend for my last year of high school. He said there was a basketball team, and that I could play ball and attend the school at no charge. I told him I would think it over and let him know. At first I thought, "No way am I leaving all my friends senior year to go to a city where I don't know anyone." But I thought about it and saw it as an opportunity to do better academically so I decided to go. I went down, did great academically, started on the team and played well. The church and leadership were great! Fellowship Church of Praise took really good care of us, from dinners to giving us jobs at the church building to keep some money in our pockets. The school- Fellowship Christian Academy took us on college tours and exposed us to some really good colleges. Because of this exposure, I attended Florida A&M University. Little did I know that one significant moment from God would push me into this much favor and purpose. We call these significant times a kairos moment.

What is kairos?

Kairos is a Greek word meaning the right, critical or opportune moment. It's a moment of favorable opportunity. In Latin, opportunity means port- when seamen would be out on the ocean & and making their way back to land and could see the shore it was all clear, it was their time to port. One of the things to note is that these kairos moments that God has for you are often wrapped in uncertainty and can even seem foolish at the time.

Favorable opportunities have expiration dates. They don't always last. Our job is to be discerning enough to know when we are in those moments and to seize every opportunity that God opens for us (Ephesians 5:16). As Jesus approached Jerusalem and saw the city, he wept over it. If you, even you, had only known on this day what would bring you peace. In other words, if you had only known the significant moment you were in (Luke 19:37-41). How are we managing the kairos that God gives us? What is hindering your yes?

Functions of A Kairos

1.) To step into your assignment.

Adam Genesis 2:15. The Lord God took the man and put him in the Garden of Eden to work it and take care of it. Training ground for the responsibility of a wife and family.

Luke 4:18- In order to step into your assignment, you have to first embrace your identity. At the onset of Jesus' ministry the first thing He did was proclaim to the world who He was and why He was sent. Every now and then remind yourself of who you are and why are here. Proclaim it out loud.

Ezekiel 8:3- God took me but the hair on my head and lifted me into the sky and in visions took me to Jerusalem to the entrance of the north gate of the inner court where the idol that provokes to jealousy stood. Luke 4:18- In order to step into your assignment, you have to first embrace your identity.

God gave temple duties & assignments based on age. Younger men had to carry heavy articles of the temple. Please do not despise your being young. The church has got to do better with recognizing, developing and deploying the assignment and purpose of God on your life. The scripture declares (Acts 2) in these last days, God says I will pour out my spirit on all people, Your sons and daughters will prophesy, your young men will see visions, your old men will dream dreams. You are valuable, you are called and chosen! Say it with me! I am valuable!

2.) To wage war, to go to battle.

For example, Caleb and Joshua had to go check out the land. There are some things you will have to fight for.

3.) To pursue your highest calling.

What is your highest calling? My highest calling is to be a minister of the gospel. I personally believe this is the highest calling of the majority of people.

4.) For God's correction.

Jonah spent three days in a whale and the children of Israel wandered in the desert for 40 years. God will discipline those he loves.

You may say, "Well, Calvin, all this sounds good, but right now I don't have any significant moments happening for me. I'm still looking for that promotion and it hasn't come yet, my boyfriend just broke up with me, my family is on the verge of breaking up.

But in the midst of this I have good news!

You can create your Kairos! Do you know what creates Kairos? Praise!

Paul and Silas were in jail and all of a sudden they began to praise! The word says around midnight Paul and Silas were praying and singing hymns to God and suddenly there was such a violent earthquake that the foundations were shaken and at once the prison doors flew open and everyone's chains broke loose (Acts 16). When you praise, chains start falling off. When you praise prison doors start opening up! When you praise there are people connected to you whose chains will start falling off! Mental, emotional, spiritual and physical chains will be broken. Hallelujah! Your praise causes a reciprocal interaction in the atmosphere and biosphere! When you praise miracles happen!

Let's go deeper into this to see how Jesus was and still is a walking Kairos moment by looking at the story of the ten men who were sick with leprosy.

Luke 17:11-19 "The Ten Lepers"

Vs. 11: Jesus passed through the midst of **Samaria & Galilee**. Anytime Jesus is passing through a place it is an indication that he is on assignment to make all things new. The word says Therefore, if any man be in Christ, he is a new creature: old things are passed away; behold, all things are become new.

Samaria– Means guardianship– What is guardianship? The position of protecting or defending someone. Being legally responsible for the care of someone. What is the highest level of guardianship? I believe it is the role of Mother and Father. Samaria had many advantages as it was in the heart of the mountains of Israel. It was also known as the "watch" Mountain.

Galilee– means circuit– to move all the way around. A route. Movement that starts and finishes at the same place. Home to Jesus and his ministry. It's where he lived and grew up. His first miracle happened at the wedding in Cana of Galilee, and his last, after his resurrection, on the shore of Galilee's sea. In Galilee, Jesus delivered the Sermon on the Mount, and the dialogue on Purity, Forgiveness, Humility and The Bread of Life. In Galilee he called his first disciples and where the Transfiguration took place.

When the Sanhedrin were about to begin with the plan to condemn Jesus (John 7:45-52), Nicodemus intervened on his behalf. They replied, "Aren't you also from Galilee? No prophet comes out of Galilee." This would be like if someone said what good can come from whatever area you are from? They did not have much regard for Galilee. Though inaccurate, because there were prophets who came from Galilee, it was a huge discredit.

I want you to see Jesus passing through Samaria and Galilee as symbolic of him walking through the corridors of your life. God through Jesus is walking in His role as Father throughout your entire life. He is walking through your past, present and future. For you he may be walking through Atlanta, Los Angeles, New York, Lagos,

Shanghai, Sao Paulo or down in Sydney. Let's go deeper–for you he may be walking through the time you were molested and the time you almost committed suicide, walking through the time you were homeless and the time you were labeled with some type of mental illness. But the good news is that Jesus is on the move and something is about to happen! He is walking from your past, into your present and He is already in your future. Jesus is not out for a casual stroll, he is walking on purpose with you in mind to heal your past, refocus your present and make all things beautiful in your future. Can you see Jesus walking?

Vs. 12: 10 men that stood afar off- Have you ever felt far away from God? Have you ever purposely distanced yourself from God? I have. There were times when I wanted to have my fun, if I'm too close you might speak a word to break up my fun. Even then it never felt quite right. Even then I knew I still needed God.

Vs. 13: Lifted up their voices- sometimes you have to lose your pride, your cool and your ego to get God's attention

Vs. 14: Go show yourselves to the priest. As they went they were cleansed.

Vs. 15: One seeing he was healed turned back and with a loud voice glorified God.

Vs. 16: And fell down on his face and glorified God, giving thanks. And he was a Samaritan.

Here we see barriers and divides being broken because Samaritans and Jews didn't socialize or get along and lepers were outcasts. But the word says he fell down on his face. The importance of this is that there are levels of praise.

7 Levels of Praise

1.) **Barak** Praise- (Kneeling Down) – means to kneel or bow and bless God.

2.) **Hala** Praise- (To Make a Loud Sound) – Halal means to be boastful. It is the root word for Hallelujah. Psalms 150. Much like fans of a sports team celebrating.

3.) **Karar**– (Dance) – Dance before the Lord like David. Psalms 149:3, Psalm 150:4.

4.) **Shabach** Praise- (A Loud Praise) – A shout unto the Lord- like when they shouted and the walls of Jericho came down. Psalm 47:1.

5.) **Thehillah** Praise- to sing, to laud comes from the word hala. Sing a spontaneous song from God. It is new and unrehearsed. Psalm 40:3.

6.) **Yadah & Toudah** Praise- (Worship with Extended hand) – Expresses Emotion, expresses praise and utilizes our hands as form of that expression. Signifies deeper surrender to God and a heart that desires to pay tribute to him.

7.) **Towdah** Praise," (The Praise of Faith) – Towdah means Thanksgiving and involves raising of hands in adoration. An attitude of sacrificial praise. Praising God before the miracle happens. Becomes a sacrifice when are in urgent need.

Vs. 17: Were there not 10 cleansed? Where are the nine?

Vs. 18: Only one came to give glory to God.

Vs. 19: Arise, go thy way: thy faith hath made thee whole.

A kairos moment is created when God finds what He is looking for. 2 Chronicles 16:9 For the eyes of the Lord run to and fro throughout the whole earth to show himself strong on behalf of those whose heart is perfect toward him. John 4:23, 24- For true worshippers worship in spirit and in truth, these are those the Father seeks. Jesus asked weren't 10 cleansed, where are the other nine? See the other nine were cleansed, but this guy was made whole because He came back to give God the highest level of praise. He came back to Barak, Hala and Towdah the Lord! He wanted to go to the extreme; he wanted to give God his best and in this defining moment not only was he cleansed but he was made whole! Not only did he see the Kingdom, he entered.

Chater 8: Lifestyle Evangelism

The I-85 Collapse

In 2017, a section of the I-85 bridge, of one of the busiest highways in Atlanta caught on fire and collapsed. Miraculously, no one was hurt or injured. After investigating, it was determined that a homeless man living under the bridge had started the fire that blazed like an inferno. I followed this story closely for weeks, and after seeing the image of the homeless man who was responsible, a revelation hit my spirit. I could see how this bizarre occurrence was symbolic of how God wants to reignite the fire of Evangelism in our lives and in this Nation. God uses some of these things to get our attention. In Atlanta & abroad, God is using certain things to get our attention and help us refocus. The bridge collapse reminds me of how God told us to go out into the streets and highways and compel people to come be with Him.

First, let's begin at the heart of the matter. It starts with a question found in Haggai 1:4 "Why are you living in luxurious houses while my house lies in ruins? Within this question we find a principle that is applicable to people everywhere: Pastors, people of God, Governors, Mayors, Presidents, citizens, cities, city council, CEOs, business owners. This is an inescapable question to all of us. Why are you building whatever your most grand idea is while the house of God lies in ruins? What is the house of God? For the people in Haggai 1, it was the physical temple built with their own hands where they could go to encounter God and worship Him. For you and I, the house of God is much different. It is not the building where we go to worship every Saturday or Sunday, but we are the house of God. Yes, walking temples, living epistles to be read of all men, possessing the same spirit that raised Christ from the dead. How is it? Christ said he would destroy the temple and rebuild it in three days. He wasn't talking about rebuilding a physical structure, He was talking about Himself. Haggai 2 mentions the latter glory of the house being greater than the former. This is also a prophecy of the Messiah and His presence in us.

In John 4, Jesus tells the woman at the well that there was a day coming where worship would not be confined to one place or location i.e. temple, church building, but the real worshipers would worship Him in spirit and in truth. So, how are we building our cities, our businesses, bank accounts, our brands, while the people of God lie in ruin: sick, dysfunctional, poverty, collapse, decay, devastation, and defeat? There could be many reasons: maybe you didn't know, thought attending Sunday church service was enough, perhaps you're too busy with your own life, too busy with church meetings and events, waiting until you have more money and resources to do anything. We all have our reasons just like the people said in Haggai 1:2 "The time has not yet come to rebuild the house of the Lord." For me, more recently it was either being too busy with my own life or waiting until I had more resources. Please understand, God wants us to build our cities, our brand, our business and bank accounts, but He wants us to do it in the right order and priority. The health and prosperity of His people is something God wants to be so in our hearts that it moves us into action. This stirring of compassion will cause the love in us to spring up, permeating every highway, every street corner, every block, every alley, every hood and every golf club community. We are the mediators of the breach! We want to be the ones to hear these words from Matthew 25: 34-36, "Then the King will say to those on his right, 'Come, you who are blessed by my Father, inherit the Kingdom prepared for you from the creation of the world. For I was hungry, and you fed me. I was thirsty, and you gave me a drink. I was a stranger, and you invited me into your home. I was naked, and you gave me clothing. I was sick, and you cared for me. I was in prison, and you visited me.'

Let's read what happens when we neglect what's on the Father's heart in Haggai 1: 3-11. Then the Lord sent this message through the prophet "Why are you living in luxurious houses while my house lies in ruins? This is what the Lord of Heaven's Armies says: Look at what's happening to you! You have planted much but harvested little. You eat but are not satisfied. You drink but are still thirsty. You put on clothes but cannot keep warm. Your wages disappear as though you were putting them in pockets filled with holes!

"This is what the Lord of Heaven's Armies says: Look at what's happening to you! Now go up into the hills, bring down timber, and rebuild my house. Then I will take pleasure in it and be honored, says the Lord. You hoped for rich harvests, but they were poor. And when you brought your harvest home, I blew it away. Why? Because my house lies in ruins, says the Lord of Heaven's Armies, while all of you are busy building your own fine houses. It's because of you that the heavens withhold the dew and the earth produces no crops. I have called for a drought on your fields and hills—a drought to wither the grain and grapes and olive trees and all your other crops, a drought to starve you and your livestock and to ruin everything you have worked so hard to get."

I have experienced losing money as the scripture mentioned. It's like having pockets with holes! As fast as money was coming in, it was going out. When I meditated on Haggai 1 and came into agreement with it, I decided to no longer keep putting my own plan before God's agenda. During that same week I received two cash offers on a home that I sensed was being hindered from selling by some unseen force that I couldn't explain. Something broke when I came into agreement with this word.

Resurgence of Evangelism

The gaping hole in I-85 was a reflection of the breach in our Evangelism ministry as the church. It gets very comfortable within the people of God to Evangelize the Evangelized, to prophecy to those who are healed, to preach to those who are already redeemed. Jesus knew we would get comfortable with this, that's why he said, "It is not the healthy who need a doctor but the sick." I have not come to call the righteous, but sinners for repentance. Those who need our ministry most are under the highways, in the streets and among all socioeconomic barriers that divide us. I-85 is an easy breach to fix, just as our Evangelism is an easy breach to fix. As soon as we come into agreement, the breach will be mended.

God wants the fire of our Evangelism to be reinvigorated, our compassion reignited and souls to be healed. There is about to be a resurgence in Evangelism! For decades we have confined Evangelism to a church team that goes out sporadically or once a month to witness to the lost. We treat it like an "add on" or put it on the back burner but it is something so much more significant and constantly on the heart of God. Evangelism is a lifestyle. In addition to going out sporadically or once a month to witness, make evangelism a lifestyle where it becomes a part of you. In his book "Lifestyle Evangelism" Joe Aldrich describes it as a way of living beautifully and opening one's web of relationships to include the nonbeliever. Evangelism is opening our lives to people. Evangelism is expressing what we possess in Christ and how we came to possess it. It is displaying God's love, His righteousness, His justice and faithfulness in everyday life. Therefore, evangelism is not a special activity that we do at a prescribed time. It is the constant and spontaneous outflow of our individual and corporate experience of Christ. More specifically, evangelism is what Christ does through the activity of His children as they are involved in:

1.) Proclamation (Psalms 96:3) – Declare is glory among all the nations, his marvelous deeds among the peoples. Sharing the good news of God's love and how that love has impacted you. Preaching , teaching, conversing out of the joy of your Salvation.

2.) Fellowship (Luke 19:5) – When Jesus reached the spot, he looked up and said to him, " Zacchaeus, come down immediately. I must stay at your house today." This is opening our world to people and having genuine community.

3.) Service (Mark 9:35) – Sitting down, Jesus called the Twelve and said, " Anyone who wants to be first must be the very last and the servant of all. Our hands must find work to do.

Keep in mind that nothing that I am mentioning here is of malicious intent, I only hope to challenge, empower and encourage. I am not singling out or specifically referring to any particular church I've visited, my current church nor any I have been a part of. This is for me first and the body of Christ. For the church in Atlanta I hear the question: Are you comfortable with just church membership transfer growth or do you also want the other people I have assigned to you? I'm not knocking membership transfer growth, it is needed, but there is another level God has for us and now is the time for us to walk into it. In the scripture below Jesus tells us to GO into the streets & lanes, GO into the highways and hedges. Throughout Jesus' ministry we see Him "going." He tells us to GO! Yet, we have become very comfortable within the four walls of our buildings. Most times when we come to God, we gradually disassociate with all our unsaved friends and family to the point where most of our friends become other church members or saved friends. In order to fully understand Evangelism, we have to note that Jesus hung out with sinners and was available to them. We have to do the same.

It's time for the church in Atlanta and abroad to shift our focus from "doing church" and "be the church." When I say doing church I mean we are so busy with church work and events inside the four walls that we stop "Going." We don't have time to make Evangelism a lifestyle, really open our lives to anyone, cultivate new friendships or make disciples because we're too busy with church meetings and events. Am I saying the church should never gather corporately? Absolutely not! However, what God designed to facilitate and amplify our worship should never replace Him. If we ever replace Him with anything, or not fully obey what He told us to do, we cause God's house, His people to lie in ruin, including those we are supposed to be ministering to and sharing our life with. We have to be amphibious, able to meet corporately in the presence of God but also able to be in the streets, workplace or wherever else with even more power, authority & demonstration. You are the church, it is not the building. The Kingdom of God is in you! When you walk up, ride up on your bicycle, pull up, or whatever, The Kingdom of God just showed up. Anything can happen! Every time you ride down I-85/75 I want you to think about how Jesus told us to go out into the streets, highways and byways. Remember how He told us to go into all the world and make disciples of all nations, baptizing & teaching them to obey all He commanded. Remember that you are the temple of the Holy Spirit. Remember how He allowed I-85 to be shut down so we could get this message & adjust. But if we are going to adjust, the first thing we have to do is get rid of our excuses.

Luke 14: 12-25

12 Jesus said to his host, "When you give a lunch or dinner, don't invite your friends, your brothers, your relatives, or your rich neighbors, because they might invite you back, and you would be repaid.

13 On the contrary, when you host a banquet, invite those who are poor, maimed, lame or blind.

14 And you will be blessed, because they cannot repay you; for you will be repaid at the resurrection of the righteous."

15 When one of those at the table with him heard this, he said to Jesus, "Blessed is the one who will eat at the feast in the Kingdom of God!"

16 Jesus replied: "A man was giving a large banquet and invited many.

17 At the time of the banquet, he sent his servant to tell those who were invited, 'Come because everything is now ready.'

18 But without exception they all began to make excuses. The first one said to him, 'I have bought a field, and I must go out and see it. I ask you to excuse me.'

19 Another said, 'I have bought five yoke of oxen, and I'm going to try them out. I ask you to excuse me.'

20 And another said, 'I just got married, and therefore I'm unable to come.'

21 So the servant came back and reported these things to his master. Then the owner of the house became angry and ordered his servant, 'Go out quickly into the streets and alleys of the city and bring in the poor, the crippled, the blind and the lame.'

22 Sir, the servant said, what you ordered has been done, but there is still room.

23 Then the master told the servant, Go out into the highways and byways and compel them to come in, so that my house will be full.

24 I tell you none of those who were invited will get a taste of my banquet."

The man who started the fire on I-85 represented the people we have become comfortable ignoring. It's the people on the highways, under the highways, lost, with all kinds of ailments, waiting on Revival. There is no condemnation or guilt I am placing on you. We are all learning, changing and growing. I honor you because you are the sons and daughters who God called and equipped for this generation to be the mediators of the breach! You have the right gifts, the right anointing, the undeniable courage and the right measure of faith to be successful. You are those who are now awakening to the call of Jesus to Go and be the ministry of love and empowerment and it will begin to flow out of an extension of who you are.

Notice in verse 21: He tells us to **go out in the streets & lanes (alleys)** and gather the poor, maimed (crippled), halt (lame) & the blind. Verse 23: He says to **go into the "highways and hedges" (barrier that separates) and compel (entreat, implore, plead, pray, ask, request) them to come in.** Instead of being descriptive again he says compel them to come in, "them" could mean more poor, maimed and halt but I also believe it could mean refugees, victims of sex trafficking & people who society have cast away. God bless some of the cities who have become "sanctuary cities" for refugees who only want to escape death in their own country and live a quality life. We cannot ignore or mistreat refugees. (Deuteronomy 10:18-19, Malachi 3:5)

Who is Jesus to You? There is a war going on over this question today just as it was when Jesus walked the earth. People are being deceived and tricked out of the faith by listening to people who don't know the answer to this question, are confused or just don't believe. Bill Faye, in his book *Share Jesus Without Fear*, gives us a great template on which we can share our faith and strategically help people to confidently answer this question and make a decision for Christ. Let me challenge you with this tough question, when was the last time someone made a decision for Christ as a result of you sharing the gospel? Yes, we must live a life before people, loving each other and walking upright to get people curious about the light they see in us, but at some point we have to directly engage people and ask them to make a decision for God through Christ.

But again I ask: "Who Is Jesus To You?" The are many who I call "extreme pro-blackers" who are "black" before they are anything else and are now allowing their hearts to become filled with hatred and almost as much racism as their former oppressors had. These are the same people who are attacking the name of Jesus and deceiving many into this doctrine. I find it very strange these same people never attack any other faith but Christianity. They don't go after Muslims or Islam but rather show respect. I ponder on the thought that the same Muslims you respect know Jesus is real. Jesus is mentioned 25 times directly and 48 times in third person in the Quran. To the extreme pro-blacker, I know you think that somehow we all believe that Jesus was blonde hair and blue eyes. This is just not true. Most of us know the Hollywood portrayal of Jesus and other biblical figures is just untrue. He had hair like wool and skin like bronze. Totally different depiction! Let's debunk another myth. Many of you think the bible, KJV in particular, was written by "the white man" and given to blacks to control us since slavery. The white man did not create the bible or faith in God and Christ. There are many versions of the bible that have been handed down for centuries, but it came from "the original text." The original text was written in Hebrew and Aramaic. The reason why we have the King James Version is because the King of England gathered scholars from all over the world from different backgrounds to interpret the "original text." After meeting together for an extended period of time, they came up with the best version in English that so closely represents "the original text." King James named it the King James Version because of this not because he wrote it. Extreme pro-blacker, my hope is that you come into the knowledge of God through Christ, the Elohim. God loves you!

All in all, put some respect on my Saviour's name. His name is Jesus, wonderful counselor, Prince of Peace, the redeemer of my soul, bright and morning star, the Son of God, the Word made flesh, the captain of heaven's armies, the One Who Was and Is and Is To Come. I believe this is the time where God will be raising up "defenders of the faith." These individuals will have the anointing, intellectual capacity to not only defend the faith but the power of persuasion. I heard a preacher say that our job is to persuade men and women into a decision. It's to sing them into a decision, to love them into a decision, to preach them into a decision.

Sometimes Jesus will test our level of persuasion. He does it when He asked Peter, whom do men say that I Am? Peter says you are the Christ- Son of the living God. Jesus says flesh and blood didn't reveal this to you and upon this rock I will build my church. Upon this rock, upon this revelation, I will build my church and the gates of hell shall not prevail against it. Jesus says I will build. Jesus builds His church. As church leaders, we should not anguish over numerical growth but rather immerse ourselves in knowing God and the ministries He has given us. As we do this, God will add to His church.

Fully Persuaded

Paul becomes like all so that he might win some over. If we are to operate effectively in Evangelism, we must understand the power of persuasion. Why did Paul choose to "become like" certain people so that he could win them over? It is because Paul understood and utilized the power of persuasion. Paul becomes like a Jew—observed the feasts, learned the Torah. To win the intellectuals, he becomes an intellectual.

He is a fisher of men. Most of the time when you are fishing, conditions have to be right on order to catch fish. For example, fishing in nature requires you to know what time fish bite the most, an atmosphere not too loud and noisy, what kind of bait are they most likely to bite on, how strong does your fishing line need to be in order to catch the kind of fish you're going after? Oh yes! It is very involved. I don't really like fishing too much but have always been intrigued by it and don't mind tagging along to carry the tackle box. But I do like being a fisher of men as it relates to Evangelism. I believe Jesus wants us to extract all the revelation we can from the metaphor, "I will make you fishers of men." We can extract some revelation by looking at the natural process of fishing and correlate it to men. So, what tools and technologies do you have in your tackle box? Let's get back to one of them that Jesus, the disciples and Paul used. It is the power of persuasion. Not manipulation, persuasion. It is manipulation when it becomes malicious intent used only for my personal gain. We use it so that God's people might have life and come to know Him. We are clear on our assignment. Jesus said to go out and "compel" men to come in—an even stronger word than persuasion, but certainly synonymous.

I remember recently feeling like I wasn't being as fruitful as I knew I could be, especially when it comes to sharing my faith and Evangelism. It's been years since I personally led someone to Christ as a result of sharing the good news with them and my testimony. I had not even made this a priority like it once was when I first accepted Christ. When I began a relationship with the Lord in October 2003, I was on fire and witnessing almost anywhere I would go. Then gradually it became less and less. Recently I had to be honest with myself and say what happened. Why aren't you on fire anymore? Why is Evangelism losing its priority in my life? Why am I not winning more people to Christ?

The truth is, though I am a believer and believe in the word of God, I had lost my conviction. A conviction is a firmly held belief, set of values or opinion. I had to take a real introspective look and conclude that I wasn't as "fully persuaded" as I once was. Not about Jesus and His Lordship, not on the bible, the gifts; those are immutable. Perhaps, I wasn't yet "fully persuaded" that I was the one for the job. I also somehow lost focus of the simple fact that time is "of the essence." We work while it is day because when night comes no man can work. Then I overall just lost focus in this area. However, I wanted this to change and I needed it to change now. So, I prayed this prayer and it went something like this: God I submit to you as Lord of my life, my life is not my own, it belongs to you. I give you a complete yes! Whatever you want me to do, I'll do. Wherever you want me to go, I'll go. Whatever you want me to say, I'll say! Use me, Lord. I'm yours!

The prayer was sincere. Instantly, I felt a fire begin to burn in my soul again, with tears rolling down my face I knew that God was giving me His fire again. Pray that simple but meaningful prayer from your heart and watch how God comes in. It's hard to burn with the fire of Renaissance & Revival when you're only "almost persuaded" or "somewhat persuaded." No, we have to be fully convinced of why we're here and how God wants to use us. Everyone's experience into how you become fully persuaded will be different, but we must be aware of what experiences God used in our lives to persuade us to run with the gospel. For Paul, his experience was very compelling. He saw a great white light, was struck blind, knocked off his horse and then heard the voice of God say, "Saul, Saul why are you persecuting me?" Paul's response: "Who Are You Lord? Instantly Persuaded! Then Ananias came and laid his hands, Paul received his sight and this was the beginning of Paul being "fully persuaded."

Paul says in Romans 8:38, "For I am persuaded that neither death nor life, nor angels, nor rulers, nor things present, nor things to come, nor powers, nor height, nor depth, nor any other created thing will have the power to separate us from the love of God that is in Christ Jesus our Lord.

There are a few things you need to be persuaded of in order to regain your confidence and get back into focus:

1.) You are the one God wants to use, yes you!

2.) If God is for you, who can be against you?!

3.) God gave His only son Jesus Christ for you, he is not withholding good from you, He wants you blessed and He has already blessed you with his best gift through Jesus!

4.) Christ is at the right hand of the Father interceding for you!

5.) Nothing can separate you from the love of Christ. Nothing!

That just freed you right there. How will you live the rest of your life fully persuaded of these blessings found in Romans 8? I see you blazing for the Kingdom of God, boldly sharing your faith and winning many into the loving arms of Christ.

Romans 4:21 says, being fully persuaded that God had power to do what He had promised. Abraham was fully persuaded that if God said Sarah would give birth, she was going to have a child despite the fact that he was about a hundred years old and she was old too. The bible says the type of persuasion or this type of faith was credited to him as righteousness. God just likes fully persuaded people. Remember He says he prefer us be hot or cold and not lukewarm.

Persuasion Techniques:

Appeal to the Supernatural- Everyone is worshipping someone or something. If you're an atheist or agnostic, you're worshipping self and your own intellect. If you're an extreme pro-blacker, you're probably worshipping your ancestors. Each of us have a desire to worship and for what is supernatural. We have a spirit, a soul and live in a body. We are spirit first. In other words, we are supernatural first. He has set eternity in the hearts of men, eternity is supernatural. Therefore, we have a longing and an inclination toward the supernatural. When the disciples had been fishing all night, Jesus told them to cast their nets on the other side of the boat. When they did it, they caught so many fish that their nets began to break. Jesus appealed to the supernatural in them. He did it to show them who He really was, to show them who they really were and so they could begin to walk in the same supernatural power! And they did!

Appeal to Reason- the appeal to reason method uses a logical argument. This method works best on people who need proof of something and don't readily accept arguments on faith more than fact. There was a disciple of Jesus named Thomas. Thomas would probably identify with one of these types. One thing I love about Jesus is that He loved Thomas enough to appeal to his logic. He is the type of God that will meet you where you are. You don't have to be perfect. Thomas needed a little extra. God gave him more than he could bargain for. Jesus tells Mary not to touch Him because he had not yet ascended to the Father, but he allows Thomas to touch Him. Why? Because this touch would be different. It would be the one to fulfill his need for logical facts that would spark supernatural faith in Thomas that was so profound.

Appeal to Emotion- is based on what a person feels. People are often led by their emotions. Emotions are feelings. Paul "became like" people to win them all because that it was a way of showing love and connecting with them. I'm more effective if you're comfortable with me.

Appeal to Trust- If people believe and trust in you, you're more likely able to persuade.

Plain Folks- People will believe you if you appear to be "down to earth." Example: A Politician says- I'm going to clean out my basement. Some people use this to manipulate through deception. But for those of us who believe, the message here is to display your humility to others. If this is truly who you are, then it's authentic and useful.

Bandwagon- If everyone believes it, it must be true. For example, if a sports team starts winning, many more people will begin to support that team. If most people like them, they must be the best. They're called "bandwagon" fans.

Rhetorical Question- A question that is not intended to be answered but rather states the obvious. For example: "Who wouldn't want to make a million dollars this year?"

Repetition- If you repeat information or present information in a repeating pattern, people will remember it and believe it.

Remember these techniques and most of all ask the Holy Spirit how and when to utilize them in your witness to other people so that you might win. Evangelism becomes a lifestyle when it becomes a part of who you are, when you start thinking of ways to reach people in your sphere of influence and begin reaching them with your light, your wisdom and truth.

Atlanta- An Epicenter of Cultural Influence

Whether it's the music where a song that "catches" in Atlanta spreads like a pandemic nationwide and then globally, or the film industry making us their new home, Atlanta has always been an epicenter of cultural influence among many other great cities in the world. I remember when Atlanta was one of the first cities to execute a plan to demolish public housing (ghettos) and provide more suitable, safer and productive living arrangements. Other cities saw how well it worked and began to implement it in their own city. After the city burned down in 1864, we built a railroad system connecting the Southeast region and rebuilt the city. We are a resilient people!

We have our strengths but we also have areas to improve. For example, are we operating with the necessary infrastructure for the amount of people we have in metro Atlanta? We have around 6.7 million people here, but do we have the capacity in our infrastructure for this density and are we planning for even more growth? Are we trying to put new wine in old wineskins? Do we put more honor on our entertainment, sports venues & teams than we do God? How is sex trafficking so ubiquitous?

There will be a great resurgence of Evangelism in Atlanta, and some of the catalysts will be from sources you never expected. Authentic relationships with Christ, transparency and healing will be happening all around. Revival will happen on the beltline while two people are riding their bicycles and talking about Jesus. All of the gifts are being unleashed from the church; you will hear prophecy on street corners. Cancer, HIV, diseases of all kinds will start being repressed and healed. Sex trafficking will be dismantled. Business owners will start to think about God's people and adjust their practices to align with the best interest of the people and what pleases Him. What happens in Atlanta does not stay in Atlanta, it spreads. Just like when you hear a song in Atlanta, you hear it in NY or Tokyo, a resurgence of Evangelism will be happening here and reverberating everywhere!

Chapter 9: Cultural Rebirth Through Kingdom Acquisition of Each Mountain

Top of the Mountains

Water and rocks don't usually flow up a mountain; they flow or fall down, unless you turn the mountain upside down! It's time to turn some mountains on their head. The word says we can speak to mountains and tell them to be moved and they would. The work of the Kingdom establishes mountains where they need to be established and deconstructs mountains where they need to be deconstructed. We will talk about how the disciples turned mountains of culture on their head, many times costing their very lives in order to establish in the earth the Mountain of the Kingdom of God.

The cover of the book has a mountain turned upside down because God is shaking up existing mountains and cultures of influence in order to establish the culture of the Kingdom. This is not anything new. He had done it before and is doing it again. In one night he turned a mountain of exploitation and systematic oppression into freedom and wealth for the Israelites. It took some force and pressure but God did it. Do you believe that God will do the same for you? I know he will! He'll turn a mountain clean upside down and make it empty out everything that belongs to you! I feel something shaking now! That mountain of death and infirmity is being shaken. That mountain of fear and disappointment is being shaken.

Depression is removing its grip off of you. I see you running into your purpose! I see every principality and worker of darkness being dethroned right now as the Lord rebukes them on your behalf in Jesus' name! I see the Kingdom of God being fully established in you!

Isaiah 2:2- And it shall come to pass in the last days that the mountain of the Lord's house shall be established in the top of the mountains, and shall be exalted above the hills; and all nations shall flow unto it. In order to understand the tremendous significance of this scripture, we must delineate the "mountain and hills" that are mentioned and their relation to culture. In their writing and teachings, Lance Wallnau and Johnny Enlow both describe how there are 7 influencers of Culture. These 7 influencers of culture are also called the seven mountains. The seven mountains or influencers of culture are:

1.) **Religion**

2.) **Media**

3.) **Education**

4.) **Family**

5.) **Business**

6.) **Arts & Entertainment**

7.) **Government**

Each culture has influence on the way we behave, the way we think and how we process information. In each one there is a reciprocal interaction, we influence them and they influence us. All of them are interconnected in some way. A problem in one of these mountains will manifest in another. In the same token, a victory in one of these will result in positive change in another. For example, if the Government raises taxes, families will be affected by experiencing a decrease in disposable income. In Arts & Entertainment, if the Super Bowl or an OTR tour comes to a city, it is guaranteed to cause a rise in revenue for local businesses—hotels, restaurants and other retail stores will see an increase in sales. God in His infinite wisdom has sent us here each with a unique gift that uses our personality, ability and anointing to influence all 7 of these cultures. Our assignment is to be a light in whichever mountain God has placed us. When this is done, we can change society and ultimately, the world.

The beauty of Isaiah 2:2 is that it describes the position of the Kingdom and Kingdom Culture as it relates to each one of these mountains of influence. It refers to the Kingdom of God being above the mountains and above the hills. The Mountains are the 7 cultural influencers, and in my opinion the hills represent subcultures derived from the 7. The Kingdom of God and Kingdom Culture is the most influential the most relevant and most powerful. For the mountain of the Lord's house to be established on top of the mountains lets us know Kingdom Culture is preeminent, the leader, the driving force which has the greater authority while everything else is a derivative. Jesus says in Matthew 28:18 I have been given all authority in heaven and on earth. Jesus' declaration here coupled with the description in Isaiah 2 gives us insight into our level of influence and authority in the culture. The mention of being positioned "above the hills" speaks of God's authority over every subculture and lets us know that all of these cultures exist within the ever expansive and eternal Kingdom of God.

The latter part of Isaiah says that not only is the Kingdom above all and within all but all Nations shall flow unto it. There is coming a day when every culture and subculture will find its way into the Kingdom. It will be a very symbiotic relationship as cultures will flow "into" and "out from" the Kingdom of God. The flow will be in to "receive and give" and out to "distribute and establish"; in to receive wisdom, encouragement, love, to give praise and honor, and out to distribute what was received and establish the Kingdom of God in culture. This is great news for all those who are citizens of the Kingdom of God. You have a message that each culture needs; you have this treasure in earthen vessels that nations cannot live without. When there is famine in your culture, you have a surplus. Where there is a lack of creativity, you are overflowing with creativity. When society is confused, debating all the issues, you have the solution. When there are people hurting and in need, you have the resources to bring them out. All cultures will flow into the Kingdom of God. I believe this scripture is the epitome of a world reconciled unto Kingdom Culture and certainly is an impetus for the writing of this book.

Kingdom Message for Each Mountain

What is the Kingdom message for each mountain?

As the earth groans for the true sons and daughters to be revealed, we have been in a time of processing. Sons and daughters are about to emerge who will have a Kingdom message specific to the Mountain they are gifted to impact. As God is processing you, it is very important that you seek to hear and understand what God is saying now for the culture you are assigned to.

Our Father which art in heaven, hallowed be thy name, thy Kingdom come, thy will be done on earth (all cultures), as it is in heaven.

Chapter 10: Reconciling The Culture of: Business, Religion and Government with Kingdom Culture

#DVP – Dreams, Vision, Passion

Imagine you're in a room, a library or office space inside of a nice home. There are custom built cabinets and shelves, hardwood floors and a desk. The only light that enters is from a large window that faces the back of the house looking out into the tall trees. There are excellent and expensive items in the room, but it hasn't been dusted in years. On the shelves are the most rare and exquisite treasures, keys and unwrapped gifts. Ironically, even though the room is full of dust and dirt from the years where it has sat empty, the treasures, gifts and keys are in pristine condition without a speck of dust on any of them.

What are these treasures on the shelf? They are our dreams and our vision.

Your dream is what you ultimately want to accomplish over your lifetime. Your vision sees everyday objectives that feed your dream. Passion is a mix of your will and strong emotions tied to your purpose that thrust you into action and pursuit of your dreams. You need all three! A person without a dream, without a purpose in life, walks around without any "pep in their step," without a burning fire in their eyes. We go through life emotionless feeling as though everything is happening to us rather than us happening to it. God is helping sons and daughters to take their dreams, vision and passion off the shelf and put them to work.

A Kingdom Message for Business

Kingdom entrepreneurs need room to grow; they can't attend every church meeting and event. We prophecy & declare millionaires but expect our entrepreneurs to neglect their business when we overextend them with church business. As soon as the church gets a person who is skilled in business, the first thing we want to do is put them on every team that we can. This is something we have to change, especially in light of the fact that they are supposed to be used by God to minister and influence the culture of Business as a whole. I have a friend who is successful in business and she asked me about whether or not she should join a team at the church. I advised her to start out as a consultant to the team first and see how that goes. I also told her to see how much of a commitment it would be and what would be required of her if she were to join the team and to ensure that it would not pull her away from conquering in business.

I believe that we should set healthy boundaries in our lives as it relates to serving within a church. Only sign up for what you know you can handle. Try not to get caught up on serving on a bunch of teams just because there is a need. When you do this something will end up being neglected because you have over-promised your time and availability. Your spouse, kids, friends, home, business and community will go neglected while you are busy serving on three teams in the church and attending every church function. This is the biggest "rope-a-dope" going on in the church right now, and it has to stop! The enemy is running amuck on every culture of influence where we should have more of a presence, but we are busy having a "shout-a-thon," attending every conference, 6 day a week church services and serving under these hierarchical systems. It seems as though you have to choose between church leadership and entrepreneurship. I declare unto you that you can be both. Jesus chose 12 entrepreneurs who were the church.

You don't have to divorce your vocation when you come into the Kingdom. If you were a businessman or woman before you come to Christ, you are a businessman or women after you come to Christ–the Kingdom of God includes your vocation. However, you must ensure that you are not putting that business before God but rather utilizing it for God; it cannot be an idol. But the litmus test for that is not determined by how many church services you go to or how many teams and auxiliaries you join. It isn't contingent on how much you give, it is contingent on your ability to discern, hear and obey God in everything.

God is looking for men and women who can successfully view their life as one whole instead of compartmentalizing. I am Kingdom at work, in the boardroom, at school, in church, on stage, in the streets. I'm the same person with the same Kingdom Culture wherever I go. Compartmentalizing is the doorway to an empty religious spirit. For example, most of us believe that only serving and working within a church context is ministry, but that is not true. Your business is a ministry as long as the vision and mission of your business is to give God a platform to use. "Seek ye first the Kingdom" also applies to when you dedicate your business to the Lord and govern it with His purposes in mind. This means you don't cheat and manipulate people for selfish gain. You are seeking first the Kingdom when you do good business!

The reason this is important is because there are plenty of Pastors and Leaders who only relate this verse in Matthew 6:33 of seeking first the Kingdom to church work and they many times condemn, convict, isolate and manipulate people who do not view it the same.

The verse does not say "seek ye first extensive, burdensome church work or perfect church attendance." It says "seek ye first the Kingdom!" Do you remember how we defined Kingdom earlier in the book? The Kingdom is much larger and tremendously more comprehensive than the church. It encompasses the church; it is above the church and in the church just like every other Mountain of influence.

Believing that seeking first the Kingdom only applies to "church service" or "church ministry" provides the template for compartmentalization. When we compartmentalize, our faith too becomes compartmentalized, causing us to lose influence. You will notice then that your gift only activates or feels the demand when you are in a church gathering or around other believers. In the church I'm a preacher but when I get to work on Monday through Friday, I'm just an employee. I don't share my faith, I'm neutral to everything. God wants us to be one whole person everywhere we go. The word says that scripture is profitable unto all things. This means wherever we are in any situation, the Word of God, the Kingdom of God has an outlet free of the encumbrances of compartmentalization. Because the word of God is hidden in your heart, and Christ the hope of glory is on you, the Kingdom of God is in you, wherever you are, and in any situation you are a living, breathing representative of the Kingdom. When you walk up, the Kingdom has just walked up, meaning anything can happen! Healing and miracles can break out, souls can be won into the Kingdom, and people can be baptized in the Holy Spirit. Implementing this revelation will cause us to not wait to get to the church gathering to express the Kingdom of God. Instead we will be an expression in every genre, every place and every influential culture of life causing Renaissance & Revival to spread all over the world.

We mentioned the Law of Reciprocity earlier in Chapter 5 and that law also applies in business. Management, Marketing, Sales and Customer Satisfaction are four functions that every business should seek to do their best in because this is the lifeblood of the business. The image below depicts how each one of these business functions: Management, Marketing, Sales and Customer Satisfaction all have a direct impact on each other. If there is an increase in customer satisfaction, there will be an increase in sales. If there is an increase in Marketing, there will be n increase in sales. If there is a decrease in Management, there will be a decrease in Marketing, Sales and Customer Satisfaction. It's safe to say that, everything hinges on management.

Management is the act of handling or directing with a degree of skill (skill is gained through training). It is to exercise executive, administrative, and supervisory direction of: a business, a family, a marriage, a church, a school, a team, an organization and the list goes on. Though it's nice, you don't need a job to promote you to manager, you're already a manager. You have the responsibility to manage all of the things I just mentioned and more. First and foremost, you have to manage your own life. I believe one area of need throughout the world is "Relationship Management." How well do we manage relationships? God is looking for great managers.

Marketing is the management of perception. How you and your business are perceived is very important. Businesses should think about how they want to be perceived. What is the story behind your business and how will you tell that story in a way that attracts your customers to connect with you? A better question is, how does God perceive your business? You are in business so that all the families of the earth be blessed. My prayer is that your business would experience unprecedented growth and success in these four areas: Management, Marketing, Sales and Customer Satisfaction.

Business Interactions

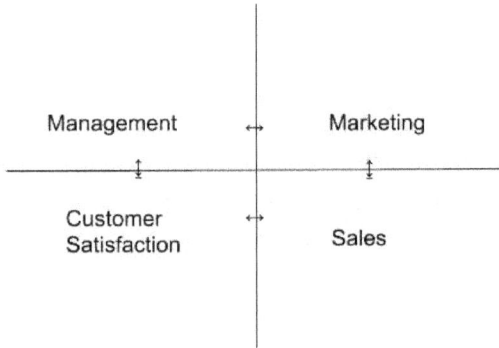

Management ↔ Marketing

Customer
Satisfaction ↔ Sales

A Kingdom Message for Religion

House of Prayer

In 2018 the Notre Dame cathedral in Paris France caught on fire and was tremendously damaged. There were age-old relics and shrines that were also destroyed by the fire. What was so bizarre to me is how within 24 hours there were donors who gave up to $700 million dollars to restore the cathedral. I quickly realized what could be the motivating factor for raising that much money. Though it is still a place where Catholics gather for mass or worship, it is currently more known for the 13 million people who visit every year for tourism. I searched online, and tickets to get into the museum or cathedral go for $11-13 per person. In other words, the Cathedral generates over 100 million dollars every year on admission alone. If this was to be a house of prayer, how did Jesus react to those who turn it into a common marketplace? He actually came into the temple, turned over the tables of the merchants and ran them out of there. He then said to them, it is written, "My house shall be called the house of prayer, but you have made it a den of thieves." If it were current day, it would be more like Jesus going into the Notre Dame Cathedral box office, driving all the cashiers out, turning over computers and crushing iPads. Moral of the story: A house of prayer is supposed to be a house of prayer, not a common marketplace. If it's no longer a house of prayer, just call it what it is—either a museum or a retail store—but don't cap off the glory and persona of God and all the relics and shrines to sell your tickets. That does not go on sale, that is something He gives to all men freely.

New Temples

I do not believe this is a random coincidence, whether done intentionally or unintentionally. I think our challenge is to really ask ourselves: What does this occurrence mean for us individually, locally and for the church at large? What is the significance? And how do we make changes? No one is exempt from the impending message.

This was a reminder of when Jesus said that He would destroy this temple and rebuild it in three days. Though he was talking about His own body, it was also huge implications for the church. As I mentioned earlier in the book, this declaration would forever change our relationship to a church building, temple, synagogue, structure or physical building. In the old system, a physical structure or temple was a large part of where and how we the church met with God, because it was where His glory dwelled. After Jesus rebuilt the temple in three days (resurrection), there was a conversion in the spirit. Our physical bodies and spirit became the temple where God and His glory dwells.

This revelation alone is supposed to transform our relationship to a temple, church building, cathedral and how we interact with them. The problem is, for the most part it hasn't, but it will. Jesus is trying to get us the "new temples," reigning, ruling, loving, ministering and influencing within various cultures of society, but we are trying so hard to stay in the building, or utilize buildings for the same purposes. Am I saying buildings are obsolete? Absolutely not. They are tools and technologies that God uses to show us His love and help us minister to people. One thing that affects our relationship to a building is the debt we owe on it, whether we're paying a mortgage or rent. Believe it or not, this also affects how we do ministry. When we have debt on buildings, there is pressure to have more gatherings at the building in order to pay for it. Then we often put more focus and attention on raising funds to pay for the existing building or buy a new one than we do to financially help the families in our congregations or the community. This burden to pay and upkeep the building often falls on the people who themselves may be struggling financially. Our relationships to buildings have to change because our current interaction with them impedes on us spreading the gospel and expressing the Kingdom. This is the next step to us moving into Kingdom Culture! We are the building, the place where the Spirit of God dwells!

Honor Women in Ministry

Women are some of the best ministers, preachers and gifts to the church and the culture. There is a verse in I Corinthians 14 concerning women being silent in church that has stirred much controversy through the years due to misinterpretation.

I believe our understanding of this is opened up when we understand the context for what Paul is saying in Corinthians and I Timothy. Context is the circumstances that form the setting. We must know the context of what was going on at the time it was written, the city and the church it was written to.

Let me start by saying Paul was absolutely supportive of women serving and leading in ministry and on occasion would honor them publicly as he did with Phoebe and Priscilla in Romans 16. We know one of Paul's assignments was to establish new churches and disciple them. As a new church they had many problems: it was chaotic, divided over leadership, disunity, sexual immorality, jealousy, doctrinal issues.

Regarding women being silent in church, Paul wrote that to the Corinthian church. Many of the women were formerly into Female Bacchus Worship; they were used to wild behavior. The name Bacchus literally means "Raving Ones," which aptly described the practices of war shouts, murderous behavior, etc. This means they were prone to yell out while someone was up teaching or loudly yell out questions. Based on the context and the fact that scripture cannot contradict itself, it is interpreted that Paul was telling the women here to hold their peace because of their past behavior which they still carried on within church. He is not a God of confusion but a God of peace. How would it look if you fellowshipped with a church and everybody was yelling out, speaking out of turn and talking over each other all while the Pastor was preaching?

Though it seems literal, I don't think the word 'silent' here means sit down and shut up. The Greek words for silent are Sigao and Hesychia. They both have a definition of also meaning tranquil, peaceable, to hold peace, still. I believe Paul is telling the women of the church in Corinthians and Ephesus to be Peaceable. New converts of Ephesus came from worshipping the pagan God Artemis (female goddess). Their ideology was female domination, over the male. Ultimately I think the scripture is telling these particular women to be peaceable, have a spirit of humility, not to yell out or talk while preaching and teaching is going on and this is the principle that lives on. I believe women are called, chosen and sent by God to be Apostles, Prophets, Evangelists, Pastors and Teachers. In many denominations, you don't see women being recognized in all five of the ascension gifts, but women have their assignments in each one as God chooses.

Line in The Sand! Who is on the Lord's Side?

The cultural climate that we are currently in is changing very rapidly. There is tension in the air as many groups are going to any length to support their beliefs–from the LGBT and gay marriage support groups, to Pro-Choice, Pro-Life, Feminists, Political, Religious and many more.

Amidst all of the debating, defaming and hysteria around the "same-sex marriage, abortion, racial issues and other divisive topics, I began to question, "What sound am I really hearing?" Then I was reminded of the scripture in Exodus 32:15-26 when Moses came down from receiving the Ten Commandments and found the people reverting to their old ways and worshipping an idol god which they had created. As Moses and Joshua were coming down from the mountain, before they could visibly see the people, they questioned what kind of sound they heard coming from the people. Was it the sound of war? It was not the sound of victory or defeat, but Moses said it was the sound of singing. In other words, a sound of people indulging in their sin with no remorse despite what God had done. I hear the same sound when I listen to what's going on and when I see what's happening, particularly with the "same sex marriage" and how some in the culture are fighting to redefine family or the abortion issue.

People are brazen and do not care what God says about this issue. Moses then openly stood in the gate of the camp and asked, "Who is on the Lord's side?" The sons of Levi responded and went on the side with Moses. Everyone else who did not move to his side came to ruin.

There's something about that egregious sound that causes indignation to rise to the point where the only question is: "Who is on the Lord's side?" That is where I am. The time has now come where we must draw the line in the sand and ask the question, "Who is on the Lord's side?" You see that line Moses drew in the sand was just as much a divider as when god parted the Red Sea so they could walk over on dry ground. When Moses drew that line in the sand it was like he was asking everyone the question, "Who is coming over to Kingdom Culture and who is staying in empty Church Culture religion? It separated those who were really willing to sacrifice from those who only wanted to *appear* as though they were sacrificing. After we have come over to the Lord's side, this means that we are not afraid of the "strong adverse reaction" that may come from the world; in fact, we welcome it, because we are not afraid of the world taking away any kind of promotion and opportunity from us! They did not give us promotion and opportunity, God did. So, it is not theirs to take away.

Do not be silent! Speak Up! Part of the reason why the LGBT and Pro-Abortion communities' strategic plans in media, politics and culture have been so effective thus far is because leaders and Kingdom citizens are not speaking up. Kingdom citizens and leaders in Atlanta, Chicago, New York, LA, Miami and around the world, I'm challenging you to speak up on this particular issue. You have been blessed with the platform and influence: speak up against the LBGT agenda to redefine family and force exposure of their lifestyle onto our children through the educational system and media. Speak up against unborn children being killed where every year almost a million babies are aborted. In the same breath, encourage someone to adopt or become a foster parent. Speak out against the injustice of racism, systemic racism, sex trafficking and the lenient gun laws! How many more key businesses, politicians, leaders, artists, trendsetters and influencers haven't stepped up and affirmed their beliefs in the public square? Is it fear of backlash? Is it fear of losing customers, endorsements, popularity, money and opportunities? You may lose some of those things, but guess what? God will restore it 7 times. The outcome is: you're blessed. If we're ashamed of him before men, He will be ashamed of us before the Father. Let us take action not now, but "right now."

A Kingdom Message for Government

Omni-Directional Prophets

I Kings 21- Elijah & I Kings 22: Micaiah

For every corrupt government there is an Elijah and a Micaiah. In I Kings 21 and 22 we see how God used them both to bring order and justice to corrupt leadership.

In the story about Elijah, Ahab, the King of Israel, saw a vineyard near his home that he wanted to purchase. So, he went and told the owner, "Give me your vineyard, because it's near my house and I want to create a garden." He also told Naboth, "I'll pay you what the property is worth." Naboth told him that the Lord forbid he give up his Father's inheritance. Ahab then went back home sad and disappointed that he didn't get the property. Ahab's wife Jezebel saw him sad and asked why he was so down. He told her, "Because Naboth wouldn't sell me the property." She then mocked him and said, "Aren't you in place to now govern the Kingdom of Israel?" She said, "Eat and be merry, I will give you the Vineyard of Naboth the Jezreelite." She then made up an evil plan and convinced the people to accuse Naboth of blaspheming God and the King. The people did just that, and Naboth was then taken and stoned to death.

Jezebel then told Ahab that Naboth was dead and that he should go take possession of the Vineyard that Naboth wouldn't sell. Ahab went on his way to take possession of the Vineyard, and in that same moment, the word of the Lord came to Elijah saying, "Arise, go down to meet Ahab, King of Israel, who rules in Samaria. He is now in Naboth's vineyard, where he has gone to take possession of it." Take notice of how this time the Word doesn't say an angel or messenger brought Elijah the message (though they could have been present), it says "the Word of the Lord came to Elijah."

As a prophet, a man or woman of God, a parent, a husband or wife, an artist, entrepreneur, or whoever you are, I pray that the Word of the Lord would come to you just as it did Elijah. I believe this is the same word from Hebrews 4:12 that is living and active, sharper than any double-edged sword, dividing joint, marrow, soul and spirit. I believe it was same presence of God that walked with Adam in the cool of the day and came looking for Adam after he had eaten of the fruit and asked Adam, where are you?

So, Elijah was hearing from God and God told him that Ahab was in Naboth's vineyard where he had gone to take possession of it. God said, "Say to him, 'This is what the Lord says: Have you not murdered a man and seized his property?' Then say to him, 'This is what the Lord says: In the place where the dogs licked up Naboth's blood, dogs will lick your blood, yes yours!' Elijah also went on to prophecy Jezebel's demise as well. Can you imagine the look on Ahab's face after hearing this word of the Lord's pending judgment for his actions? It was judgment for Ahab, but vindication and justice for Naboth's family. It is also important to note that after Elijah prophesied judgment to Ahab, Ahab humbled himself. The word says, "He tore his clothes, put on sackcloth, fasted and went around meekly. God took notice of this and asked Elijah if he noticed how Ahab had humbled himself. Because Ahab had humbled himself, God didn't allow disaster to hit right away. But Ahab would likely never have had an opportunity to humble himself if he had only received words of victory and success and if no one had been bold enough to look past his title and speak the word of the Lord. Needless to say all of the words God spoke through Elijah came to pass.

Before Ahab's death, he and The King of Judah, Jehoshaphat, were inquiring whether they should join forces to fight a war against their common enemy, Syria. In an effort to make the decision, they gathered 400 prophets together at the town gate to give them a word on whether they would have victory and success if they chose to battle Syria. The prophets one by one began to prophesy Victory for Israel. They said, "Go up, the Lord will deliver Syria into our hands." After all the unanimous prophecies of 'Go, it's ours,' Jehoshaphat said, "Is there not a prophet of the Lord we can ask?" Ahab said, "There is one named Micaiah, but I don't like him because he always prophecies against me," so they sent someone to bring back Micaiah to ask him.

So, both of the kings sat on their thrones at the gate of Samaria while all the prophets began to speak. We have to take notice of the gate. The kings sat on their thrones at the gate. Prophets prophesied at the gate. The gate represents the epicenter of government, business, trade, commerce, technology and culture, out in the general marketplace among the people. Elijah, Micaiah and so many others did not confine their prophecy to those who were in the synagogues in contrast to many prophets today who only prophesy within a church meeting. We see Micaiah prophesying at the gate of Samaria. We also see the false prophets prophesying at the gate of Samaria. Part of the problem in today's culture is that most of the false prophets are speaking at the city gates, areas of heavy traffic in the culture, while the prophets of God are within the church meeting. Prophets of God, we need you in the city, in the economic, spiritual and cultural center of it all. There is a place for you at the forefront.

When Micaiah finally arrived and they asked him if they should go to battle, Micaiah said that he saw Israel scattered like sheep on a hill without a shepherd. "They have no leader, let every man return to his home in peace." Micaiah then said the 400 other prophets had lying spirit; they got upset with him and one false prophet smacked him in the face. Micaiah urged them to listen, but they didn't and decided to go to war anyway. Well, the words of Micaiah came to pass, as did the previous word of Elijah concerning Ahab when he died in battle.

Do prophets prophesy to powerful leaders anymore? For example, do they prophecy to Apostles, Presidents, Kings, Prime Ministers, Pastors, Mayors, Governors, CEOs, Artists, Actors, and Influencers of Culture? We need prophets like Micaiah who won't be coerced or bribed to only prophecy success and victory to those in leadership but to speak only what the Lord tells them to speak. I think many churches do a phenomenal job with prophetic training. It is absolutely a need and I commend any church for taking time to cultivate this gift in the church. Normally when undergoing prophetic training, we have heard throughout the years that we only prophecy in three areas: edification, exhortation and comfort.

Recently, I began to question this statement, not the validity of the men and women who may have said it (because they are great men and women), but the statement itself. Yes, we do prophecy edification, exhortation and comfort because it is what God uses to bring healing on a deeper level. I do think a believer should master being able to do prophesy in this capacity. However, when we look in scripture we see prophets speaking on a wide range of things, not just edification, exhortation and comfort. We see them speaking a hard truth, to sharing a warning or an unfavorable outcome, revealing wisdom in an area, giving God's decision in an area.

I had known all along that prophets spoke on a wide variety of subjects, but after I read about Micaiah, I felt it was impressed upon me to think about this differently. I wondered, are we raising up prophets in the body of Christ to be like the worldly prophets for hire that only prophecy success and victory when we teach them to only prophecy edification, exhortation and comfort, or are we raising up prophets to be like Micaiah who speak only what the Lord speaks? This is one of the signs of a true prophet and a Kingdom Principle, because Jesus said "I only do what I see the Father doing and I only speak what the Father speaks."

Edification, Exhortation and Comfort is only half the story; it is time for full disclosure. Full disclosure is when you tell it all and leave nothing out as the Lord leads. I believe that when we teach prophets to only prophecy edification, exhortation and comfort we are laying a foundation for them to become "victory and success" only prophets. I think we have to evolve that teaching into also admonishing them to "speak only what the Lord speaks." Yes, we absolutely need to know how to speak words of healing and comfort, but ultimately we speak what God speaks.

Do you remember the earlier teaching in Chapter 4 about harnessing the wind? You had the traditional windmill that could only catch wind from one direction, and the other was omni-directional. Prophesying in one area is "one directional." Speaking what God speaks is omni-directional. God needs the omni-directional prophet! I'm reminded of the omni-directional wheel in the middle of the wheel that Ezekiel saw. I believe those wheels represent many functions, processes and cycles of the Kingdom of God. The wheel could go in any direction without turning—North, South East and West. Think of the tremendous acceleration this wheel accomplishes.

I also believe this wheel can travel through dimensions—the dimensions of past, present and future. When we think about travel, dimensionally it is very easy for the mind to conceive the present and future. But why would this wheel or even God need to travel to the past? Great question! For the most part, we have a linear experience with time where it moves on a timeline that we have to think of as going back to the past. But God, who is outside of time, has a different perspective on the past. I don't believe He has to go back to the past but that He is in the past, present and future simultaneously. How do we come to this reasoning? If you remember in scripture when Adam and Eve were removed from the Garden of Eden, the word says cherubim were placed there with flaming swords to guard the entrance. This is significant because the place still exists, a living tangible place. For us it seems to be in the past, but not God; He is still there. Now fast forward to the cross where Jesus gave his life, died, was put in a tomb and resurrected. For us it seems to be in the past, but I believe it opened up a place in the spirit realm that still exists today and love and healing power and grace are still flowing right now from the place where blood and water flowed down and the place where they rolled away the stone to find an empty tomb.

The word says His blood cries out from the mercy seat. What is the blood of Yeshua saying to God? I believe it is saying, "Have mercy on them, forgive them, these are your beloved sons and daughters, remember your promises concerning them, and bless them with your right hand!" I believe that every miracle performed in the word opened up a place in the spirit realm by God that are like pockets of grace and favor that we can tap into by faith. There is about to be a rise of "omni-directional prophets" who will Go where He says Go, Speak what He says Speak and Do what He says Do. The word says there will be many false prophets to arise and even some of the very elect (meaning believers) will be deceived. Here are some ways to discern a true prophet:

1.) Speaks what the Lord says to speak.

2.) Does what the Lord says to do.

3.) Goes where the Lord says to go.

4.) Is Christ-like.

5.) Driven by a desire to please God.

6.) Displays the fruit of the spirit.

7.) Their words come to pass.

Two types of prophets: one directional and omni-directional. (Creative illustration courtesy of Belinda Jackson for "Picture it Possible").

Where are the prophets who will prophecy judgment if the Lord says judgment, victory if the Lord says victory? Where are the prophets who will prophecy to gangs and drug dealers on the street? Where are the prophets who will prophecy to the homeless and the Leaders of Nations? I believe a new boldness and authority is about to arise in sons and daughters to prophesy to systems and structures; archaic and oppressive systems and structures that have been in operation for centuries are about to be shaken up! They are about to get a Word from the Lord. For many, it will not be an appeasing word, but it will be necessary and cause a great re-order, demolition, reconstruction and realignment.

Let the whole world sing for joy because you govern with justice and guide the people of the whole world. (Psalms 67:4). Unfortunately, our songs of joy come and go in waves. Sometimes we get justice, sometimes we don't. Sometimes there are laws created that benefit the people, sometimes they don't. Right now our songs have been turned into frustration and anger because our government is practicing "selective justice." If you live in this zip code, subscribe to this social class, come from this certain ethnic group, then there is justice for you. But if you are a young black boy in Orlando, Florida walking home from the local store with some of your favorite goodies–Arizona iced tea and skittles–in your comfortable hoodie only to be harassed and killed by a wannabe community cop, there is no justice for you. The day Trayvon was killed and the day his murderer, despite all of the evidence at hand, walked out of the courtroom with impunity was yet another shameful day in American History for our justice system and the government. I believe the blood of Trayvon Martin still cries out to the Lord from the ground. It is crying for justice and for an America where this would never happen, much less be tolerated. Though man's natural law somehow let the murderer go free, keep in mind spiritual law supersedes man's law. Just because you get away with it in man's law does not mean you have escaped. Spiritual law says you reap what you sow and vengeance is the Lord's. It is time for there to be a revival in government where we implement laws that reflect Kingdom Principles.

"Unto us a child is born and the government shall be upon His shoulders." (Isaiah 9:6). The shoulders are the place of burden and responsibility. In other words, the government will be his responsibility, the place of His purpose and assignment, leadership, authority, power and management. What government is Isaiah referring to? It is undoubtedly the government of God, also known as the Kingdom of God. Jesus' assignment for coming was to establish this Kingdom in the earth. The government of God is already established in heaven; Jesus came to establish it in the earth, show us how it is to be established and make disciples to sustain and extend its' establishment. How do we know? Verse 7 says His government and its' peace will never end. He will rule with fairness and justice from the throne of His ancestor David for all eternity. Later after Yeshua's arrival to fulfill this prophecy of Isaiah, he would make the declaration, "Thy Kingdom Come, thy will be done on earth as it is in heaven." All of heaven is committed to the establishment of the Kingdom of God, the government of God being established.

Faith & Values -vs- Separation of Church and State

Separation of Church and State is not a law, it is a paraphrasing of Thomas Jefferson in his description of our first amendment protection that "Congress shall make no law respecting an establishment of religion, or prohibiting the free exercise thereof." I don't think the paraphrase "separation of church and state" is really the best one to use given what the law intends to do. First, it intended to protect religion, not just the church. So I could see "separation of religion and state" or better yet "non-intervention of state with religion" as a more applicable paraphrase. The first amendment was given to protect religious freedom so that we don't become like an authoritarian government that tells people who they can and cannot worship. America did not want to become that, thus we have the First Amendment. So it's less about an actual separation and more about protection of religious freedom.

Furthermore, the government, through Congress, passed a law so I could have the recognized freedom by the states to practice my "religion." That law is still active because Congress upholds it, so where is the separation? Whenever a conversation comes up about the involvement of Faith, Church, Religion or just including moral values into Government and Politics, one of the first knee-jerk responses I hear is "you know there is separation of church and state." In other words, you can't expect politics to do anything moral because there is separation of church and state. I hear the "separation of church and state" argument especially when it comes to abortion. What I want women everywhere to know is whether you have had an abortion or have considered it and you have asked God's forgiveness, you are forgiven. God has given you grace and mercy so you don't have to walk in guilt or condemnation. For those women who are beating their chest in pride saying it is my body and my choice, I hope the reality sets in that it is murder and not something we as a country should be proud of. The lives of unborn babies need a voice too, and that is their voice in Congress. They will have millions more once people stop embracing the guilt, embarrassment and fear to speak out brought on by the culture.

I am happy the "heartbeat bill" was enacted. This is a bill that makes abortion illegal once a heartbeat is detected. After reading the bill, I understand that the penalties fall more on the physician than the woman. People love to debate the justification for abortion being women who were raped, incest or complications during pregnancy when studies show that those rare instances account for less than 5% of abortions performed in U.S. The fact is 95% of abortions are done because people simply decided they didn't want the burden or responsibility for whatever reason. Instead of any plan, debate or solution whatsoever, for the 95%, they will debate the 5% tooth and nail. For any one woman who went through rape, incest or had complications, I pray God's healing for you. If this is the case and you are deciding whether or not to keep the child, keep in mind that God will help provide for you, the child and the family. As a society we can help prevent the 95% by teaching self-discipline, responsibility, implementing God's principles and love for life. We need more solutions on how to help all women who are facing the decision to become a mother—abortion is not it. The word says I knew you from before, formed you and knit you together in your Mother's womb (Psalms 139).

There may be a separation of religion and state but there has never been a separation of Faith, Values & State. Why? It is because all people have Faith and Values and these are what guide what they believe and how they act. Faith and Values influence what policies people create and the implementation of them. This is why there is such a tug of war. Members of the LBGTQ community want policies for their values. Pro-Life and Pro-Choice groups hold a tug of war based on what they believe. Gun law people do the same for what they value. I personally think there should be tougher gun laws. There are too many mass shootings at schools and public places, and the laws need to change this immediately! But you see the tug of war in government and politics because of "Faith and Values." It's all about what a person has faith in and what they value. I certainly do not believe that "separation of church and state" implies that people have to walk into Congress as an empty shell and leave their faith and values at home. It is the opposite: Government wants people who have Faith and Values. Those who are in the Kingdom of God and people in general have a responsibility to influence policies with our Faith and Values that are inspired by God. We will not be told it's "separation of church and state, go sit over there and be quiet while everyone else boldly influences policy with their Faith & Values." Quiet season is over; it's time to be like a raging storm to influence policy with our Faith and Values.

Chapter 11: Reconciling The Culture of Media, Arts & Entertainment and Education with Kingdom Culture.

A Kingdom Message for Media

Media is defined as the main means of mass communication: broadcasting, publishing, and the internet, collectively. I think media culture as a whole has to rediscover its "why" and return to values that enhance the quality of life for its audience. In order to do this, we have to ask the question why does Media exist? Media exists to educate and to entertain. If it is to educate, let it be education that builds the community up and not reporting that continues to stir up division. Keep in mind people have died because of the lies and excessive reporting you did on things that were not beneficial for our community. For example, the East Coast vs West Coast beef. You operated as a tool of destruction instead of the life giving conduit you were purposed to be. If you're going to entertain me, let it be something that gives me a genuine sense of humor. Don't grab my attention to let me know of the latest scandal and gossip you have so earnestly dug up with the intent to destroy a reputation and boost your ratings. Report the whole truth and not a sound bite that fits the narrative you want to portray. Report what is true. Report what you can prove. Rediscover your why. Your purpose is to be a conduit of good news and information that all the families of the earth be blessed.

A Kingdom Message for Arts & Entertainment

Let's acknowledge Elohim throughout the entire creative process, not just at the awards ceremony. If we acknowledge God throughout the process it will not allow the content we produce to be steered by a set of values that are not founded on Kingdom Principles. As creators we are "driven" or inspired by many things. What is driving your creativity? The answer to this question will determine the type of art, film, music, product or service you produce.

We see in Arts and Entertainment the slow and gradual seduction to infuse everything with the LBGTQ lifestyle. As popular in mainstream culture as it is trying to become, Jesus came to the conclusion that the Lesbian and Gay (LBGTQ) community might be healed and saved. People who are a part of the LBGTQ community have been through a lot of pain, and in many cases are from torn relationships and broken families. My prayer is that God would heal their hearts. I love the LBGTQ community and want to see them healed and walking confidently in their God given identity. I have had conversations with individuals who identify as LBGTQ and some of them will say they feel they were born that way. My response is that it's quite possible to feel born and drawn to the same sex when you think in terms of what is handed down through the transcription of DNA.

My college friend from FAMU who is now a doctor, studying to find a cure for cancer gave me an in-depth lesson on how DNA is transcribed. He explained to me that many habits—from what we eat to what action we take every day—can be transcribed on our DNA. For example, if you eat candy and sweets often, it gets transcribed onto your DNA, causing your body to remember it so that now you naturally crave candy and sugar. If you smoke cigarettes, the same thing happens. If you enjoy healthy activities, it gets transcribed on your DNA and becomes a part of your make-up. If it becomes a part of your DNA, it can be passed down to your children. With this transcription of DNA proven in science and confirming what the word of God says about how iniquitous patterns are handed down from generation to generation, it is easy to see how a person can feel gay or lesbian from a very young age. Those feelings have been handed down to you from some of your ancestors who may have participated or struggled with it in their lives. Just because you feel it doesn't mean it's you. You are not a sin or a mistake but the decision to alter or mutate your identity is. If you have made a change in your identity, you can still be saved through faith in Jesus Christ.

The challenge then becomes: will you accept those feelings as "it's just who you are," or will you shake them off and embrace your identity as the man or woman God originally made you? I saw you shaking the LBGTQ feelings and lifestyle off like Paul shook off the snake that bit his hand. The snake will come to bite every generation, it's what you do after being bitten. In other words, not even just about those who identify as gay or lesbian, the feeling will come for every person to do something contrary to Kingdom Principles; it's what you do after those feelings come. Some people get bit and choose to stay bit. They wallow in self-pity, rejection, confusion and pain, while others see it for what it is and "shake it off." Shake those feelings of being gay, lesbian, transgender off and come into the identity of who God made you as His son or daughter. God was not confused and He did not make a mistake. You were wonderfully made from the beginning and God loves you.

Then there is the issue of exploitation. For the people in power who see talent as something to exploit rather than a gift to be shared with the world, this has to change. Or, because you are the "gatekeeper," their fee of entry involves some type of exploitation, I'm talking to you. Men have got to stop exploiting or mistreating women for sexual favors. It is not right! Other men should confront them and discourage that type of behavior. This is a selfish action that does not express love and has no place in the business of Arts & Entertainment. On the same token, women have got to stop selling sex or sexuality at whatever level they are on. As far as the "me too," movement I think there are many women who have actual experiences with sexual assault and who have been hurt that my heart goes out to because they deserve better. However, there are many women who were willing participants in their exploitation and then cry about it later and file all these lawsuits to embezzle millions, tarnishing the legacy of men. This practice is not right and the "me too" movement women should confront those women and discourage them from this unscrupulous activity.

These latest cultural events lead us to the conundrum that awakens our consciousness to the resolution and the reason I wrote this book. I find it peculiar how "Arts & Entertainment," including "Hollywood," praises sexual exploitation in film, in art, on stage and in music, but want to renounce it in reality. You can't have it both ways. If it's worth renouncing in reality it's definitely worth renouncing in the content of your creation of film, in art, on stage and in music. We are now beginning to awaken to yield to God's culture while fully established within our culture. I say "fully" because in Arts and Entertainment we may acknowledge God, but do we acknowledge him in "all" of our ways? Our attitude prior has been, 'God I accept the ideas, inspiration, the creativity but you can keep your thoughts on sexuality and indulgences, they're a little too rigid for my liking.'

"Culture Vultures" is a term I first heard from a famous music industry executive Dame Dash, and it exists in many facets. Vultures eat on things that are dying. Could it be that it's not because of the Vultures that the culture is dying, but because the culture has tried to exist so long apart from its Creator? It has tried to sustain itself and gradually became distant from Kingdom culture being the first culture established in it. It's just like if I tried to continue to use my iPhone without the electric powered battery and never recharged it. My iPhone can do a bunch of amazing things that its creator designed it to do, but apart from power, it's inoperable. Kingdom Culture was the first operating culture established. Sticking with the same example, Apple uses the iOS system for all of its products whether it's the iPhone or iPad, the operating system is the iOS. Similar to how iOS is the operating system for the iPhone, Kingdom of God culture is the operating system for every individual and every culture of influence. When we choose other operating systems like ones that exploit each other through drugs, sex, violence and other detrimental things that are not Kingdom of God culture, we swing the door wide open for Culture Vultures to come in. The change starts from within.

Kingdom Message for Education

Culture of Education, you must seek to extract the highest and best from everyone you encounter. In doing this, it will require for you to seek to understand what potential lies beneath the surface. The same route may not be for every student so we have to incorporate options that play to the strengths of each student instead of expecting them to thrive in a set system that may not be their strength. For example, every child may not want to attend college. Some may want to start a business after high school or work in a skilled trade. How are we setting these students up to thrive when this is their strengths as a student? Is there any high school curriculum that include learning a skilled trade or how to start a business? It would be a great idea if schools incorporated more classes like these into their curriculum. How about learning social media marketing while you're in high school or a class on real estate investing? There needs to be more classes that prepare students for adult life after high school. It would be great to have classes on how to manage finances, use bank accounts, pay bills and maintain good credit.

I also want to see education take a stand for our kids. You do not have to accept a change in your culture just because there is a change in another. For example, a change in family culture where there are two moms or dads, transgender parents etc. does not mean you have to begin adding to your curriculum a change in the definition of family and teaching this. It also does not mean you have to allow transgenders to have story time with our children. You do not have to begin teaching kids that they have a right to choose their gender.

What should be incorporated into the history books is the rich history of African Americans before slavery, how we were Kings and Queens owning our land, using agriculture and being prosperous. Then we can teach the rich history of Native Americans before the Thanksgiving feast with the Pilgrims and Christopher Columbus. Tell the true story of how Native Americans occupied the land first. The purpose of education is to set one's mind free. It is like planting a seed, watering it and watching it grow.

Chapter 12: Reconciling The Culture of Family With Kingdom Culture

Kingdom Message for The Family

In His vision for culture, the church, civilization and ultimately nations, the first thing God did was create man, woman and a family. See what great love the Father has lavished on us, that we should be called children of God! And that is what we are! The reason the world does not know us is that it did not know him. Dear friends, now we are children of God, and what we will be has not yet been made known. But we know that when Christ appears, we shall be like him, for we shall see him as He is (John 3:1-2).

The first thing to know is that God has a tremendous love for family. As you can see it says what great love the Father has "lavished" on us. Family is the crown jewel of His creation and God wants us to experience here on earth the magnitude of this great love.

For those who are led by the spirit of God are the children of God. The spirit you received does not make you slaves, so that you live in fear again; rather, the spirit you received brought about your adoption to sonship. And by him we cry ABBA, Father. The spirit himself testifies with our spirit that we are God's children. Now if we are children, then we are heirs—heirs of God and co-heirs with Christ, if indeed we share in his sufferings in order that we may also share in his glory (Romans 8:14-17).

In order for humanity to experience the full weight and magnitude of this love we have to lead by the spirit. It is the spirit of God that lets us know what love is and helps us to begin to understand it. Just as God has adopted us as sons and daughters, it is a Godly, loving act to adopt other children into our families. Because the families in our countries are broken, the foster care systems are overcrowded and broken. There was a wise lady who told me that if every Christian household adopted one child in foster care, it would end the need for the foster care system in a single day. How beautiful would that be? I long for the day that we realize this dream.

So Christ himself gave the apostles, prophets, evangelists, pastors and teachers to equip his people for works of service, so that the body of Christ may be built up until we all reach unity in the faith and in the knowledge of the Son of God and become mature, attaining to the whole measure of the fullness of Christ. Then we will no longer be infants, tossed back and forth by the waves, and blown here and there by every wind of teaching and by the cunning craftiness of people in their deceitful scheming. Instead, speaking the truth in love, we will grow to become in every respect the mature body of him who is the head, that is, Christ. From Him the whole body, joined and held together by every supporting ligament, grows and builds itself up in love, as each part does its work (Ephesians 4:11-16).

The purpose of family is to represent Christ in the earth and produce a generation who has cultivated Kingdom of God culture. God desires for families to be blessed beyond what you can imagine. In Genesis 22:17-18 God tells Abraham I will surely bless you and make your descendants as numerous as the stars in the sky and as the sand on the seashore. Your descendants will take possession of the cities of their enemies, and through your offspring all the families of the earth will be blessed, because you have obeyed me. I believe that every family should have a written Mission statement, Vision statement- detailing their values and family goals and objectives. These family goals should include wealth goals. Most other things in life we give attention to detail except to when it comes to one of the most important assignments in life and that's family. For our business, we spend hours creating a business plan, marketing plan, networking and strategizing so that company can be successful. But how much time do we spend planning and strategizing so that the most important entity of marriage and families will be successful? Starting today, sit down with your family and write down 3-5 goals for your family and what action steps you will take to accomplish them. Sit down with your spouse and write down 3-5 goals for your marriage as well. Talk through your purpose, ask the question why does your family or marriage exist and what do you want to accomplish? Ask the Holy Spirit for the answers. When the Spirit answers or when you know the answer, write it down. You will use those answers to create mission and vision statements and your family goals and objectives.

Restoration of Families

God is sending a strong wind of reconciliation to come upon families. The wind is coming for Fathers and Sons, Mothers and Daughters, Fathers and Daughters, Mothers and Sons, Husband and Wives. The relationships are going to be mended on the deepest level causing families to be healed and strengthened. Strong families make strong communities so you will begin to see communities and cities being transformed. In his book, "One Flesh – The Winning Team: A Practical Guide to a Happy, Healthy, and Lasting Marriage," Dr. William Ekane takes us into a comprehensive look at God's intent and design for marriage and families. The book also speaks of the restoration that is in store for families.

There is going to be significant healing in the relationship between Fathers and children. Fathers are coming back into the household. The demonically instituted narrative "I grew up in a single parent home," is about to be rewritten. This narrative has been weaponized against us for decades. For some it has been translated into a badge of honor for the Mom and the child. Why? For one, families historically and still today are awarded benefits of housing and food stamps if the man was out of the home. So here it is a government welfare program to keep the man out of the household in order to be taken care of by government. This was demonically instituted and what helped produce this narrative I spoke of earlier. Some of you may say well, I never lived in the projects. Well, keep in mind a climate sustained creates culture. Many of us are one generation or less away from being in a family who lived in housing projects which started in 1934. They were started post American Civil War Reconstruction era (1863-1877) and pre Civil Rights movement (1954-1968), but they still exist today in many states. From these dates you can see that some cultures like these have been in place for decades and even centuries. The effects of these are still being felt today in many families. Regardless of if you experienced it firsthand or not, the culture of this thing has to be broken. You are a part of breaking it and establishing a new culture of family.

The narrative is about to be rewritten. Let me share with you what helped me realize this. I grew up in a single parent household for half of my childhood and on to adult life. Just for me hearing that narrative so much and even beginning to say it myself, I think I subconsciously began to reinforce the invisible wall between my Dad and I that was already there. I masked what I was feeling even more and acted like my Dad was less needed. I did that by not calling, being distant and holding unforgiveness in my heart. Looking back as I've gotten older, I realize that at whatever, capacity, willingness or ability he could provide, I needed that. Whether it's a phone call every now and then, or hanging out whenever, I needed that. Sometimes the anger, frustration and bitterness of what is not being done destroys the relationship between both parents and the children. I kept focusing on what was not being done and on all the negative instead of all the good that God had placed in my Dad. One day I chose to let go of all my hurts from what was not being done and in that moment I forgave and started to heal. It was only then could I truly celebrate and accept the capacity in which my Father was able to give me. The relationships with my Mother and Father are healing, growing and still evolving. I thank God for them and my entire family; they are a blessing in my life. My prayer is that through you all the families of the earth be blessed and that your family is blessed.

Femininity and the Feminist

"You can love your femininity without being a feminist."

Feminists and Feminism is a way of viewing your femininity to a very extreme level, which leads outside of Godly boundaries. First off, when you see "ist" on the back of something it already gives it an impression of seeming to communicate that it is superior. What if I said I was a "masculinist?" Wouldn't you think that I was trying to portray that being masculine is superior to anything else? Look at the term "White Nationalist" and you see my point. Feminism first appeared after Adam and Eve ate the fruit of the tree of knowledge of good and evil and as a result the scripture says the woman will try to rule her husband. In more recent times, feminism was born out experiencing the boundaries of social inequality, where women did not receive equal pay in the workplace nor were they treated equally. I think women deserve equal rights, pay, honor and acknowledgement. However, that is not justification to cast off all restraint. Godly boundaries are still needed. What would the earth be if the sea had no boundaries? Where would the earth be if it had no boundaries on how close it could get to the sun? Godly boundaries are in place because you are loved.

Yes, you have the power of choice, but your body is meant for sexual relationship with a man, not a woman. I think women do deserve equal rights, pay, honor and acknowledgement.

Yes, you were given a body but you do not have the right to kill unborn babies.

Yes, you are equal to a man, but you are not to think you are better than him. (Neither is he better than you.) I always remember this line from one of my favorite singers, "You don't have to hate the men to stand for women."

Chapter 13: New Church

New Church

It is very unfortunate what happened to the passengers and staff of the two 737 Max planes that crashed in 2018 within five months of each other. My heart goes out to their families. One was Ethiopian Airlines and the other was Lion Air. One report said that the plane came down only minutes after it took off. A wonderful crew from Ethiopia lost their lives. It is our prayer that God strengthen and comfort the families of all who were lost. The reason why the plane went down is because there was a new software system installed whose job is to stabilize the plane when the nose of the plane seems unbalanced. This system will automatically tilt the nose of the plane in a downward position as an attempt to balance. The name of the plane is the 737 Max. It was originally built in the 1940s, and over the years the 737 Max has been modified to make upgrades and changes. The plane had been recently renovated to include this new technology that attempts to stabilize it like an "auto correction" type of function. As the plane took off the pilot noticed that the nose of the aircraft kept "auto correcting" itself in a downward position, but the problem is they didn't need a downward nose because they were taking off, not landing. They were in the ascent, not descent. The pilots frantically tried to override the software and manually correct it by trying to pull the throttle in a complete upward position. However, the auto correct function of the new software never relented and continued to drive the nose of the plane downward until it eventually crashed.

This would be the second 737 Max to crash under the same or similar circumstances. After this incident the FAA grounded all Boeing 737 Max planes in an effort maintain aviation safety, uncover the problem and prevent anymore fatalities. Officials began a thorough investigation of why both of the planes crashed. They eventually came to the conclusion that the new software along with other issues in the inherent design of the plane was the culprit. It was concluded that more training for the pilots on the new software was needed. But there was a more comprehensive dilemma in the explanation as to why both of the 737 Max planes crashed. It has a 50 year old design. Over the years the 737 Max kept undergoing revisions to its style and design, but the problem is the design was completely outdated. For example, the engines are so low to the ground—only a minimum of 17 inches above the runway, when newer planes have a minimum of 28 to 29 inches. This problem alone could cause a plane to explode on contact if the pilot lands wrong; the engine should be higher up off the ground to avoid any potential problems. Investigators said the 737 Max kept revising an old design when they should have created a new airplane design decades ago. Did you hear me? They said continuous modifications to something that should have been completely made new was the ultimate reason why the planes crashed.

I immediately saw the correlation with the church and other influencers of culture. We are continuously trying to revise broken and outdated systems. Jesus said, "Behold, I make all things new." This is why many of us have felt the "mundane burden" that makes us restless even when we are trying to do things differently. I have felt this way too as a new Pastor trying to lead a church differently, and we actually did different "out of the box" creative stuff, but something still didn't feel quite right. After a while, I still felt it would become a routine and not what my spirit could identify as the total will of God for me. Sometimes we are trying to renovate an old wineskin to make it fit. Maybe if we get a new logo, or renovate the building with the most state of the art equipment, maybe instead of calling it Hallelujah night we call it Invasion of Glory. Maybe if I put my mixtape out too and talk about how much lean I drink, If I show more skin and more of my body (not naked though but in workout clothes), maybe then my product or service will sell. Instead of doing the work for our marriage to stay together, let's just be the best co-parents we can be and move on. Or, let's be the best co-parents but not divorce and get nice and comfy in a dead marriage. All of these are unnecessary revisions to an already broken system that God wants to make new.

New Structures, New Systems, New Wineskin

I believe the reason some of us pioneers and creatives become restless and annoyed is because we know there is more but we haven't found the sweet spot. The reason we haven't found the sweet spot of God's perfect will for each and every one of us is because in many cases we are trying to revise, renovate, rehab and modify an old system or structure. Every now and then when you're riding through the hood of Atlanta you see old houses built in the 1930s that have been completely renovated. This is where they kept the same initial structure but just added all new upgrades, and they are immaculate. Next door to that same house that is renovated you may find an investor who chose to demolish the old house from the 1930s and build something totally new, and they're phenomenal. Now is the time to get into the new! We often fall into rehabbing old systems because they are handed down to us from those who have authority and influence with us. The burden is placed on us to keep it going and take it further. This has been an issue for generations and is now one for millennials as baby boomers age and are divesting and implementing successors.

It would be like if David after Saul gave him his armor decided to find a tailor to make the structure of Saul's armor fit instead of just giving it back. Some systems are not tailored for you, just give it back and stick with what God gave you. Because in the old system we have been trained never to question the authority, desires, ideas or requests of the man or woman of God, many of us do actually tailor

Saul's armor and try to live life, do ministry and everything else with it on. I don't believe David had an opportunity to be indoctrinated with that type of empty religious culture because he was too busy out back tending to sheep, alone with animals, his song and the presence of the Lord. It was David's rejection that worked as a shield against the old system and structure being able to take root in his heart. Did you know that even your rejection is working for you? Empty religious culture did not have a chance to discourage the realization and utilization of his own authority. If it had, David would have said, "Okay, Saul, whatever you want me to do," and it would have certainly cost Israel the victory. But no, David, full of the spirit of the living God, confident in his authority, told Saul he could not use his armor and would fight the new way—the unconventional way that defies the status quo and does something that was not new to David but new to his generation.

It is time for the New Church! Jesus said, "Behold, I make all things new!" Also when speaking to the woman at the well who was seeking clarity on where to worship, Jesus said to her a time is coming when you will worship the Father, neither on this mountain nor in Jerusalem. But an hour is coming and is now here when the true worshippers will worship the Father in spirit and in truth. God is spirit and those who worship Him must worship in spirit and in truth. He did not say those who worship must worship in a building at 11am Sunday and Wednesday at 7pm. He didn't say there was a set attire or set ways like we often see in man's religious culture. The set prerequisite is that it's done in spirit and in truth.

The traditions of men make the gospel to no effect. I believe this is true primarily because once it becomes a tradition or routine of man, this replaces the requirement of it being done in spirit and truth. Does that mean everything being done is not of spirit and truth? No! But it does mean the fullness and overflow of what could be happening is being inhibited. What are the traditions of men being practiced right now in our generation that is limiting the gospel? The one I believe it to be right now is the Sunday morning at 11am and Wednesday 7pm in the same building every week. This is also known as the institutional or traditional church. For example, we're trying to put the new things that God has given us into the 9am and 11am service and it just doesn't fit because it cannot contain it.

I don't believe what I'm about to say applies to every single church, because God still has a need for the traditional church and many people still have a need for it. However, there are many of us builders, pioneers and creatives that are called to step into the new day that Jesus mentioned to the woman at the well. We get agitated when coming to the same building at the same time every week. Something in our spirit knows there is more for us to do and we know that "more" will be done outside of the building. However, our partnership, love and collaboration with the traditional church will remain because we are all still one church with different functions. The new church will be uninhibited by a building and will utilize them with the proper perspective. The new church will not involve empty religion, spectatorship and mundane routines. The new church will merge application technology, faith & ministry to make it possible for people all over the world to meet at different places, different times for different reasons but "One" purpose. There will be small, medium and large groups meeting together outside the church building but still being the church. The new church will harness the power of the omni-directional wind and it will be a place where Kingdom culture is established.

The New church will create new ways to get ministry into their communities. The new church is intentional and sincere about creating and maintaining friendships. Unlike the empty religious culture of traditional church where pseudo-friendships and connections are made with the intent of numerical church growth, the new church will value organic, authentic relationships being cultivated with no ulterior motive to gain new members so we can reach a numerical goal to stroke our ego. Not everyone who has a numerical membership goal is seeking to stroke their ego, many just want's God's church to be powerful and influential, but there are others who have these goals with wrong motives. Authentic friendships will thrive in the new church because the motive is to be friendly because we want friends. We want friends because we value and need one another; two is better than one and we truly believe we can do more together. Iron sharpens iron and we understand that we need each other in order to be the best versions of ourselves. I remember a time when I had a steady workout partner in the gym. As I think back over it now, I was in the best shape of my life when my friend and I were constant workout partners. Friendships like these will create strong communities and make disciples.

Chapter 14: Renaissance and Revival

All Nations

Though we have 7 continents and around 7 billion people on earth, All Nations are really two groups: Those in the Kingdom and those who are not, those who put God's culture above their own, and those who do not. All Nations refer to the various nationalities and multicultural people who will be separated into one of those two groups. This word ultimately helps us understand how God perceives the world as one whole even though there are 7 continents with gigantic oceans that divide the land. I believe this shows us that God sees it as one, but because of our limited knowledge, perspective and understanding we often have a hard time viewing the world as a whole.

Here is the scripture that supports my definition of "all nations." Matthew 25:31 says "When the Son of man shall come in his glory, and all the holy angels with him, then shall He sit upon the throne of his glory: And before him shall be gathered all nations and He shall separate them one from another, as a shepherd divides his sheep from the goats. And he shall set the sheep on his right hand, but the goats on the left. Then the King shall say unto them on his right hand, come, ye blessed of my Father, inherit the kingdom prepared for you from the foundation of the world."

Mark 13:10- And the gospel must first be published among all nations- The chapter starts out with one of the disciples admiring the beauty of the architecture, stone works and elaborate buildings. Jesus turns to him and says not one will be left on another. Peter then asks Jesus when will the city be destroyed, what signs will happen? Jesus starts naming all of these bad things that would happen, nation against nation, kingdom against kingdom, disciples themselves would be persecuted and then He says and the gospel must first be published among all nations. We could interpret it as Him saying before things get really bad and before I return in power and glory to gather those that are mine the gospel must be preached among all nations. I like the use of the term "published" from the word kerysso which means preach, proclaim, herald like a public outcrier. Who will be doing the publishing? It is you and I because we are living epistles to be read among men. The gospel has to first be published among all nations because Renaissance and Revival is for all nations.

Isaiah 2:2- And it shall come to pass in the last days that the Mountain of the Lord's house shall be established in the top of the Mountains, and shall be exalted above the hills; and all nations shall flow unto it. The time is here where all the nations of the earth are flowing unto the Kingdom of God. We are needed in this hour for divine solutions and strategies for our world. Every culture of influence is coming to us for wisdom, insight and direction. There is a famine in the land. There is a famine of publishers. Those who will write as God says write it, say it how God says say it and do it as He instructs to do it. Because God is pouring out His spirit so profusely, that famine is changing into plenty. Every culture of influence will flow into the Kingdom of God culture and I'm excited about it!

Renaissance and Revival

The word Revival comes from the word revive which means: to live, to have life, sustain life, to cause to grow, be restored to life or health, from sickness, from discouragement, from faintness, from death. Live prosperously, restore, refresh, repair, a restoration to use, a restoration to acceptance, a restoration to activity.

Starting now I'm expecting Revival to spring up in your life, in mine and across the world. It will look like new and ancient wells being discovered and restored. We will find our place of bethel, ancient places of worship, gates of heaven, our place of rest. It will look like signs, miracles and wonders, families restored, healing and deliverance ministry and cultural transformation. I'm also seeing Renaissance, which we defined earlier as a cultural re-birthing. For the cultural transformation to take place I think each culture needs to learn from each other. For example, what if the church could learn the loyalty seen in the music culture? What if Family culture could learn the discipline found in Education culture? What if Business and Government could learn the integrity found in Kingdom culture?

We started with Church Culture because church culture has to be aligned in order to influence the other cultures. Therefore, church culture and every culture—Family, Religion, Media, Arts & Entertainment, Education, Business, Government—will be reconciled with Kingdom Culture.

In this place we will see that He is the God of Renaissance and Revival!

Diagrams

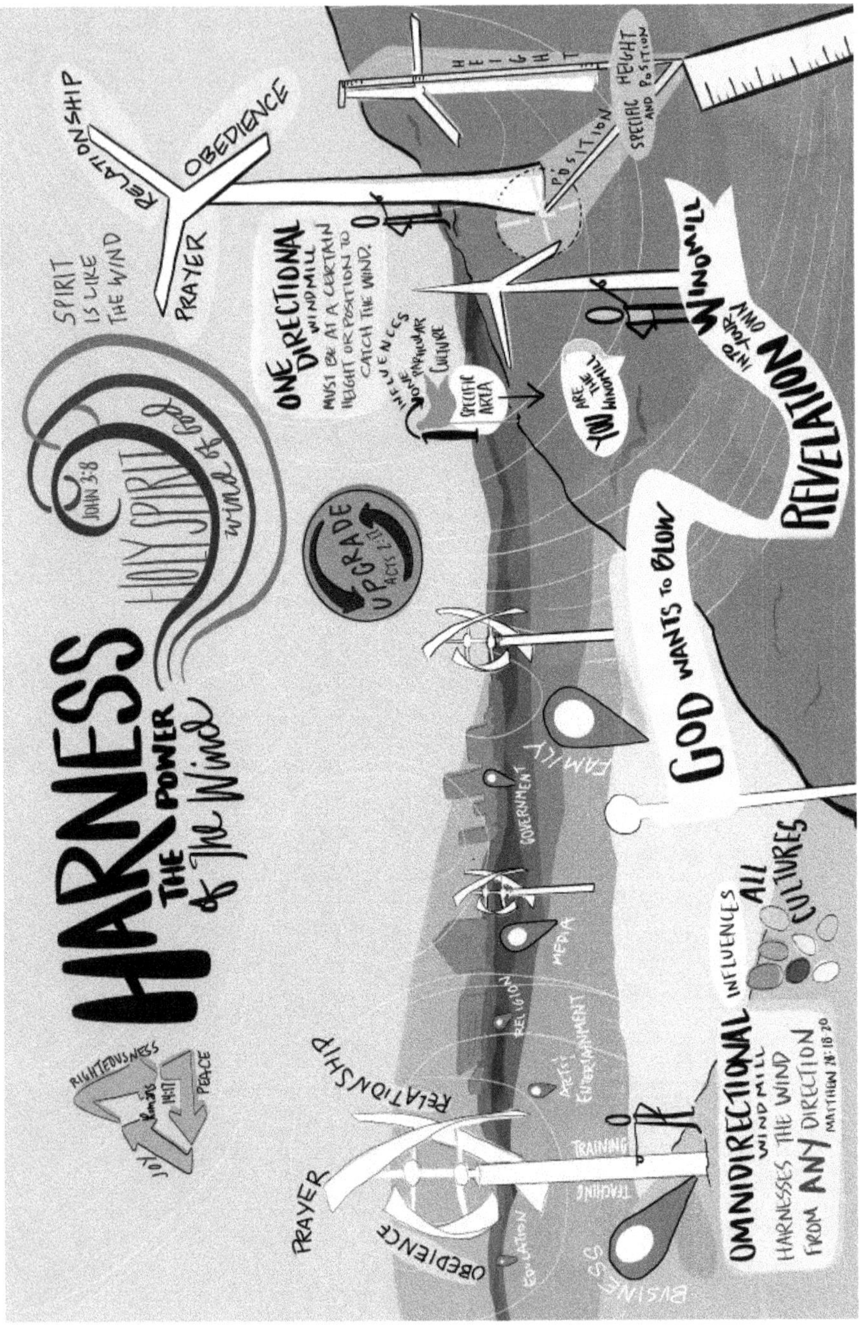
HARNESS THE POWER of the Wind
HOLY SPIRIT
JOHN 3:8
wind of God
SPIRIT IS LIKE THE WIND
RELATIONSHIP
OBEDIENCE
PRAYER
UPGRADE ACTS 2:17
ONE DIRECTIONAL WINDMILL
MUST BE AT A CERTAIN HEIGHT OR POSITION TO CATCH THE WIND.
INFLUENCES ONE PARTICULAR CULTURE
SPECIFIC AREA
YOU ARE THE WINDMILL
HEIGHT
POSITION
SPECIFIC HEIGHT AND POSITION
GOD WANTS TO BLOW INTO YOUR OWN WINDMILL
REVELATION
RIGHTEOUSNESS
PEACE
JOY
PRAYER
RELATIONSHIP
OBEDIENCE
EDUCATION
BUSINESS
TEACHING
TRAINING
ARTS/ENTERTAINMENT
RELIGION
MEDIA
GOVERNMENT
FAMILY
OMNIDIRECTIONAL WINDMILL
HARNESSES THE WIND FROM ANY DIRECTION
MATTHEW 28:18-20
INFLUENCES ALL CULTURES

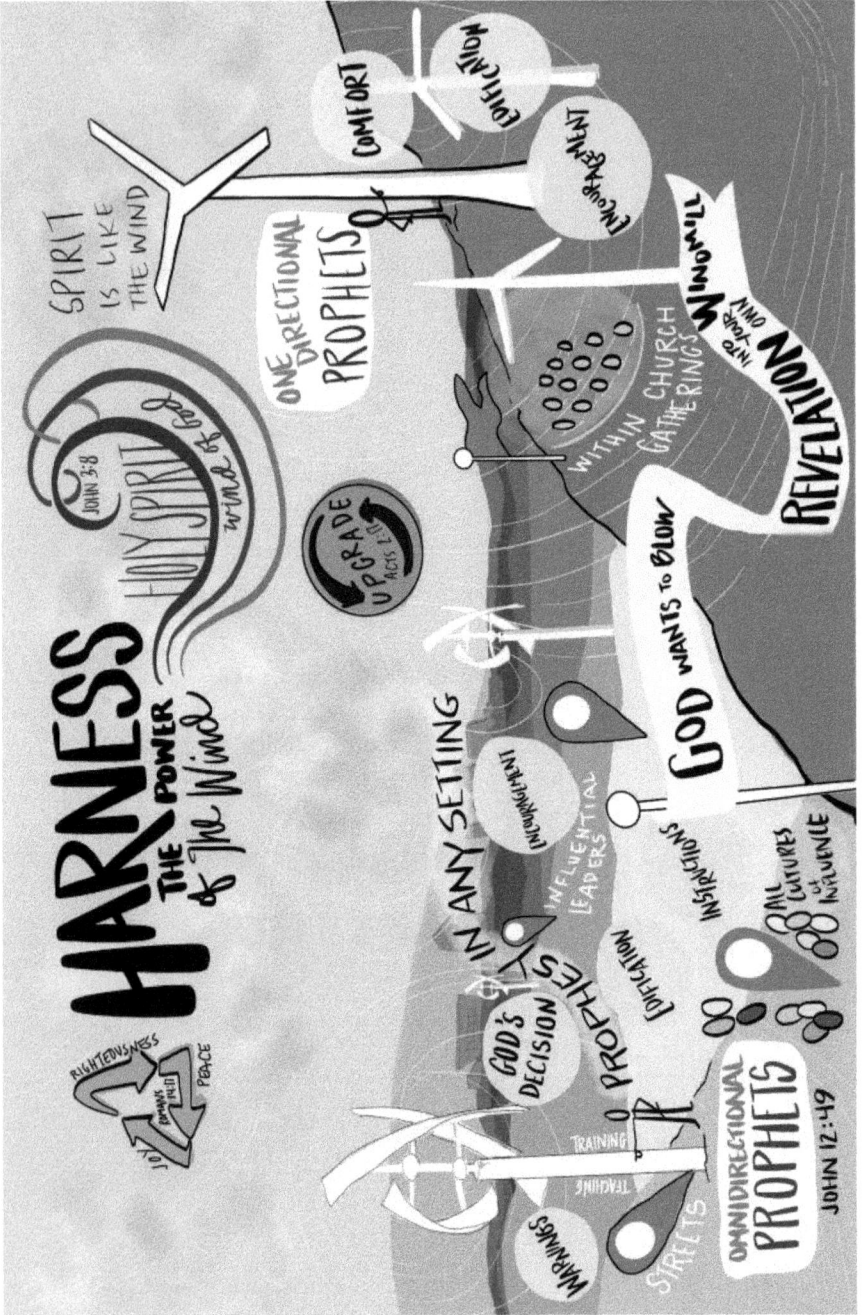

4 Spheres of Earth Interactions

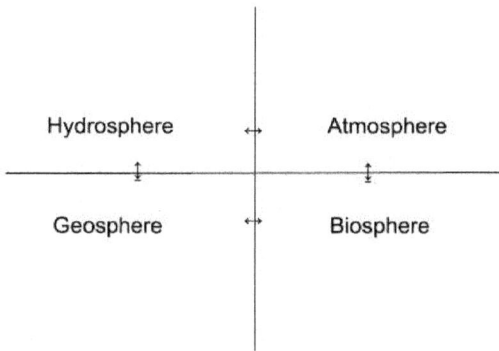

Hydrosphere ↔ Atmosphere

Geosphere ↔ Biosphere

Business Interactions

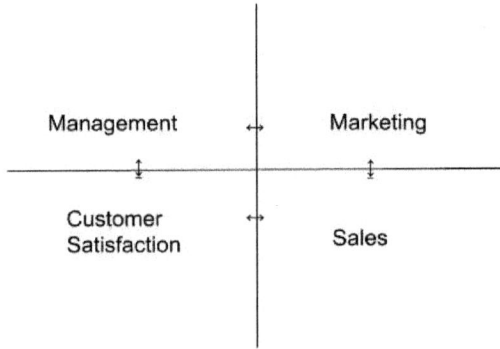

Management ↔ Marketing

Customer
Satisfaction ↔ Sales

Notes

References

Graham Cooke and Gary Goodell. (2006). "Permission Granted To Do Church Differently In The 21st Century."

Richard L. Reising. (2006). "Church Marketing 101- Preparing Your Church For Greater Growth. A Revolutionary Blend of Corporate Marketing Strategy and Biblical Wisdom."

Paul Viera. (2006). "Jesus Has Left The Building."

Johnny Enlow. (2009). "The Seven Mountain Mantle – Receiving The Joseph Anointing To Reform Nations."

Dr. Philip R. Byler. (2008). "The Changing Church in the Unchanging Kingdom."

Bryan Meadows. (2013). "Dirty Knees and Green Thumbs – A Guide To Planting The Extraordinary and Seeing The Impossible Grow."

Joe Aldrich. (1981). "Lifestyle Evangelism – Learning To Open Your Life To Those Around You."

William Fay and Linda Evans Shepherd. (1999). "Share Jesus Without Fear."

Joanne Goddard. (2017). Interrupted To Intercede – Challenging You To Embrace The Divine Disruptions In Your Life."

Dr. William Ekane. (2017). "One Flesh – The Winning Team. A Practical Guide To A Happy, Healthy and Lasting Marriage."

William L. Seymour. (2000). "The Doctrines and Discipline of the Azusa Street Apostolic Faith Mission of Los Angeles, California."

Mark Miller. (2011) "The Secret of Teams – What Great Teams Know and Do."

Bryan Meadows. (2018). "School of Revival."

Dr. Matthew Stevenson. (2019). "Road To Romans" Message Series:

-) "Confronting Critical Christianity."
-) "The Full Gospel."
-) "Holiness Is Not Hard."
-) "The Technology of Preaching."

William Kamkwamba, Chiwetel Ejiofor,. (2019). "The Boy Who Harnessed The Wind." – Netflix original movie.

Zenovia Andrews. (2014). "All Systems Go – A Solid Blueprint to Build Business and Maximize Cash Flow. Surely There Is A More Consistent Way To Do This."

T.D. Jakes. (2017). "SOAR! Build Your Vision From The Ground Up." Message- "The Power of One."

Tiphani Montgomery. (2019). "God Is My CEO" VLOG Messages.

Paul David. (2003). "Kingdom of God & Kingdom Culture Teachings."

David and Vernette Rosier. (1993). "Equally Yoked – Keys To Effective Family Ministry."

Jonathan and Amanda Ferguson. (2019). "Living In The Spirit." Episode 1 & 2.

Kanye West and the Sunday Service Collective (2019).

Ron Kenoly. (1992). "Righteousness, Peace and Joy" (in the Holy Ghost). (song).

Paula Price. (2006). "The Prophet's Dictionary – The Ultimate Guide To Supernatural Wisdom."

James Strong. (1995). The New Strong's Exhaustive Concordance of The Bible.

NIV & KJV Bible.

Strong's KJV touch bible app.

www.biblegateway.com.

www.biblehub.com- Benson Commentary.

www.ingramcontent.com/pod-product-compliance
Lightning Source LLC
Chambersburg PA
CBHW071436090426
42737CB00011B/1673